2A

Math in Focus®

Singapore Math®
by Marshall Cavendish®

Workbook

Consultant and Author
Dr. Fong Ho Kheong

Authors
Chelvi Ramakrishnan and Michelle Choo

U.S. Consultants
Dr. Richard Bisk, Andy Clark, and Patsy F. Kanter

Marshall Cavendish
Education

U.S. Distributor

Houghton
Mifflin
Harcourt

© 2015 Edition Marshall Cavendish Education Pte Ltd

Published by Marshall Cavendish Education
An imprint of Marshall Cavendish Education Pte Ltd
Times Centre, 1 New Industrial Road, Singapore 536196
Customer Service Hotline: (65) 6213 9688
US Office Tel: (1-914) 332 8888 Fax: (1-914) 332 8882
E-mail: cs@mceducation.com
Website: www.mceducation.com

Distributed by
Houghton Mifflin Harcourt
222 Berkeley Street
Boston, MA 02116
Tel: 617-351-5000
Website: www.hmheducation.com/mathinfocus

First published 2015

Math in Focus® Workbook 2A
ISBN 978-0-544-19382-6

Printed in Singapore

16 17 18   1401   23 22 21
4500816402   A B C D E

Contents

Numbers to 1,000

Addition up to 1,000

CHAPTER 3 Subtraction up to 1,000

Using Bar Models: Addition and Subtraction

Multiplication and Division

CHAPTER 6
Multiplication Tables of 2, 5, and 10

CHAPTER 7
Metric Measurement of Length

Mass

Volume

Name: _____ Date: _____

CHAPTER 1 Numbers to 1,000

Practice 1   Counting

Write the numbers shown by the base-ten blocks.

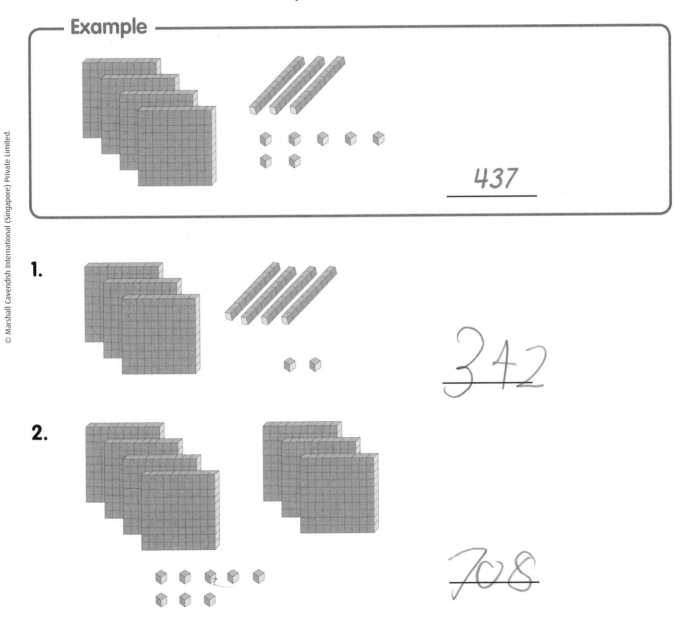

Example

437

1.

342

2.

708

Write the numbers in words.

Example

1,000 — one thousand

3. 999 — ninehundred ninety-nine

4. 420 — fourhund twenty

5. 615 — six hundfifteen

6. 704 — Seven hundred four

7. Fill in the chart with the correct numbers.
The first one is done for you.

  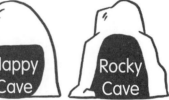

three hundred thirteen	*313*	C
six hundred six	606	P
five hundred fifty-five	555	O
nine hundred twenty-four	924	H
three hundred six	306	W
four hundred fifty-eight	458	A
one hundred ninety-nine	199	E
six hundred sixty	660	R
seven hundred twelve	712	N
three hundred thirty	330	V
eight hundred seventy-two	872	Y
two hundred eighty-one	281	K
five hundred forty-three	543	S

Write the letters that match the numbers.
Find which cave the train is going to.
An example is shown.

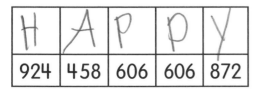 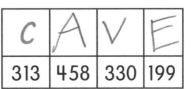

H	A	P	P	Y
924	458	606	606	872

C	A	V	E
313	458	330	199

Find the missing numbers.

8.

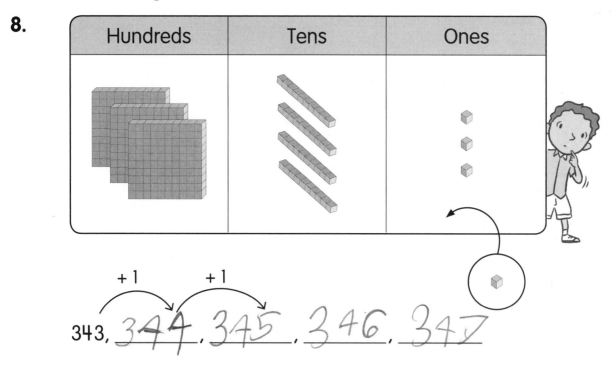

Hundreds	Tens	Ones

343, 344, 345, 346, 347

9.

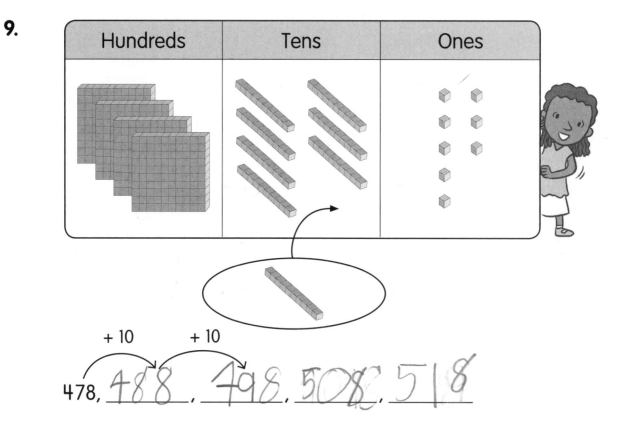

Hundreds	Tens	Ones

478, 488, 498, 508, 518

Find the missing numbers.

10.

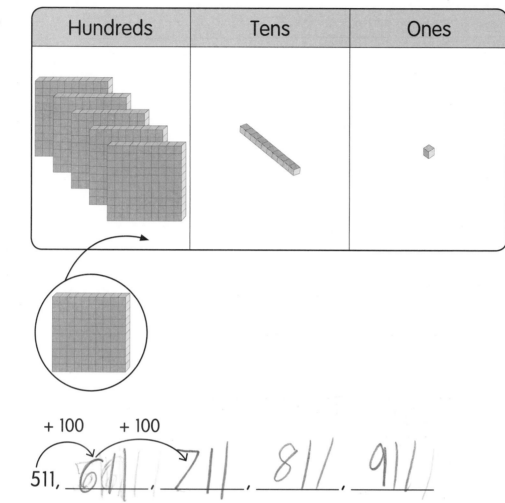

Hundreds	Tens	Ones

+ 100   + 100

511, _6̲1̲1̲_ , _7̲1̲1̲_ , _8̲1̲1̲_ , _9̲1̲1̲_

Freddy Frog loves to count.
Count with him and find the missing numbers.

11.

203   204   205   206   207   208

Freddy Frog loves to count.
Count with him and find the missing numbers.

12.

13.

14.

Practice 2   Place Value

Look at the place-value charts.
Then write the numbers in standard form, word form,
and expanded form.

Example

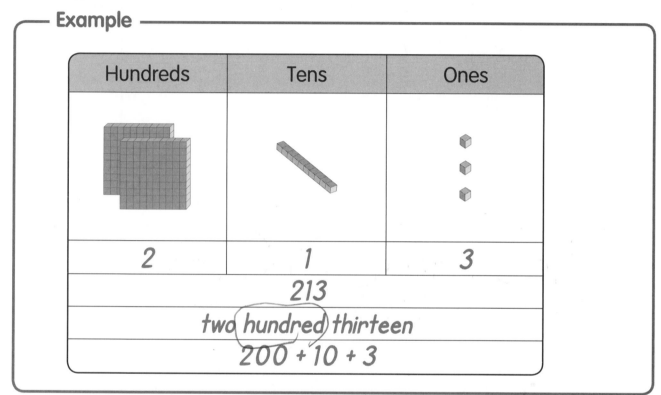

Hundreds	Tens	Ones
2	1	3

213

two hundred thirteen

200 + 10 + 3

1.

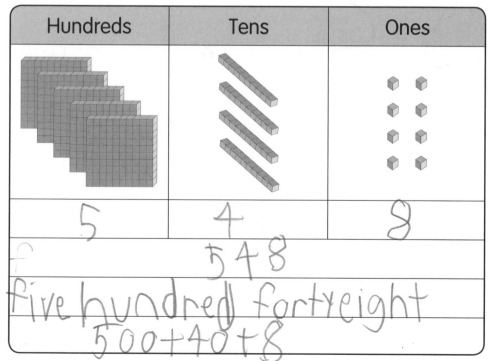

Hundreds	Tens	Ones
5	4	8

548

five hundred fortyeight

500 + 40 + 8

Write the numbers in standard form, word form, and expanded form.

2.

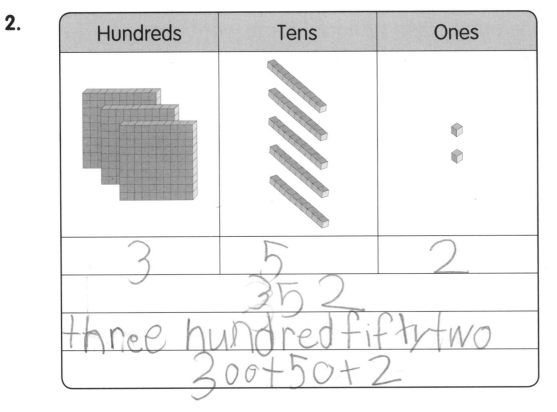

Hundreds	Tens	Ones
3	5	2

352

three hundred fifty two

300 + 50 + 2

3.

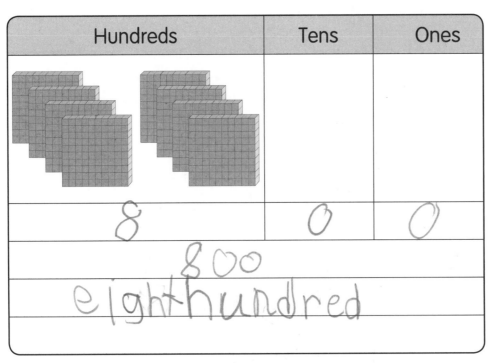

Hundreds	Tens	Ones
8	0	0

800

eight hundred

Write the numbers in standard form, word form, and expanded form.

4.

Hundreds	Tens	Ones
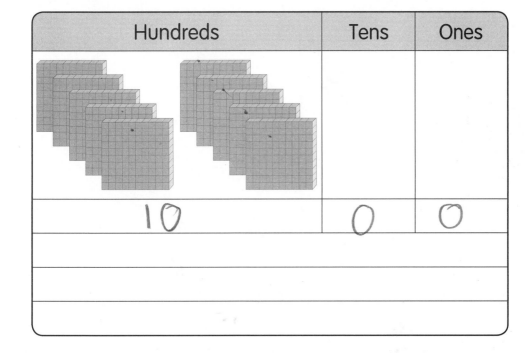		
10	0	0

Write the missing numbers and words.

Example

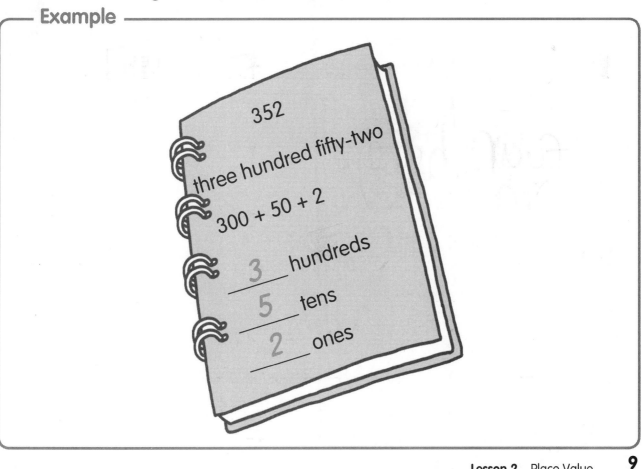

352

three hundred fifty-two

300 + 50 + 2

__3__ hundreds

__5__ tens

__2__ ones

Write the missing numbers and words.

5.

694

Six-hundred nineter four

600 + 90 + 4

6 hundreds

9 tens

4 ones

6.

901

nine hundred one

900 + 0 + 1

9 hundreds

0 tens

1 one

7.

719

four-hundred nine teen

400 + 10 + 9

404 hundreds

1 ten

9 ones

Name: _____   Date: _____

8.   **Color these bubbles.**
Use the same color for bubbles that show the
same number.

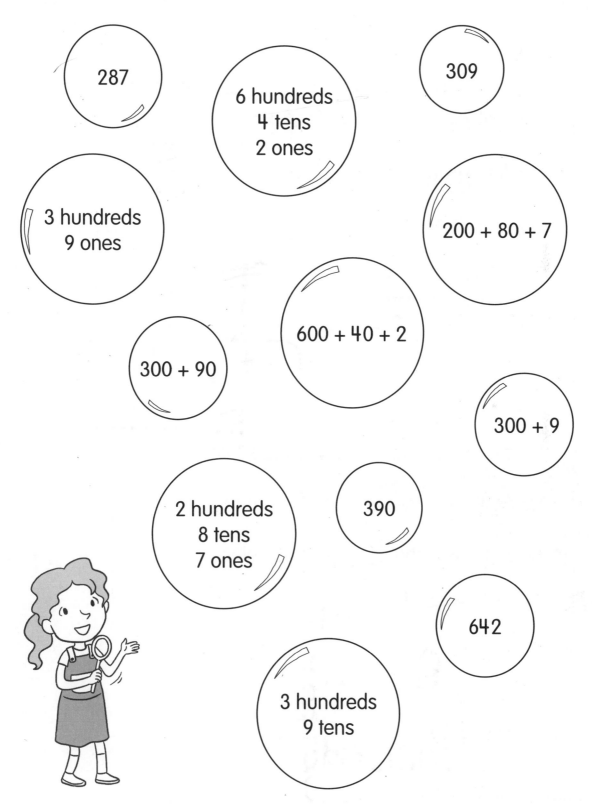

287

6 hundreds
4 tens
2 ones

309

3 hundreds
9 ones

200 + 80 + 7

300 + 90

600 + 40 + 2

300 + 9

2 hundreds
8 tens
7 ones

390

642

3 hundreds
9 tens

Read the number.
Write *hundreds*, *tens*, or *ones*.

9.

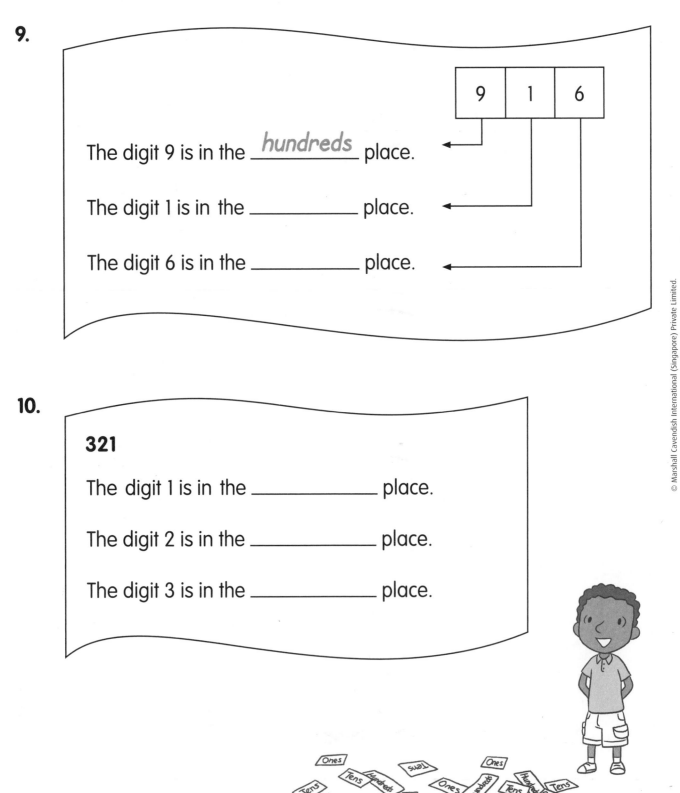

| 9 | 1 | 6 |

The digit 9 is in the _hundreds_ place.

The digit 1 is in the _____ place.

The digit 6 is in the _____ place.

10.

321

The digit 1 is in the _____ place.

The digit 2 is in the _____ place.

The digit 3 is in the _____ place.

Practice 3 Comparing Numbers

Write **greater than** or **less than** in the blanks.

— Example —————————————

256 is ___*greater than*___ 246.

First compare the hundreds.
If the hundreds are the same, compare the tens.
If the tens are the same, compare the ones.

1.

118 is ___less than___ 181.

2.

595 is ___less than___ 959.

Compare.
Write > or < in the ◯.

— Example —————————————

555 (>) 550

Write > or < in the ◯.

> means greater than.
< means less than.

3.

1,000 ◯> 100

4.

789 ◯< 897

5. Write *T* for true or *F* for false.

55 is less than 455.   F

355 is greater than 455.   f

400 is less than 455.   F

450 is greater than 405.   F

800 < 809   F

980 < 809   f

89 > 98   f

863 > 862   F

Practice 4   Order and Pattern

Order the numbers.
Use the place-value chart to help you.

1.

	Hundreds	Tens	Ones
214	2	1	4
457	4	5	7
590	5	9	0

_823_ , _810_ , _794_
least

2.

	Hundreds	Tens	Ones
810	8	1	0
794	7	9	4
823	8	2	3

_828_ , _810_ , _794_
greatest

3.

	Hundreds	Tens	Ones
361	3	6	1
348	3	4	8
607	6	0	7

_348_ , _361_ , _607_
least

4. Order the numbers from least to greatest.

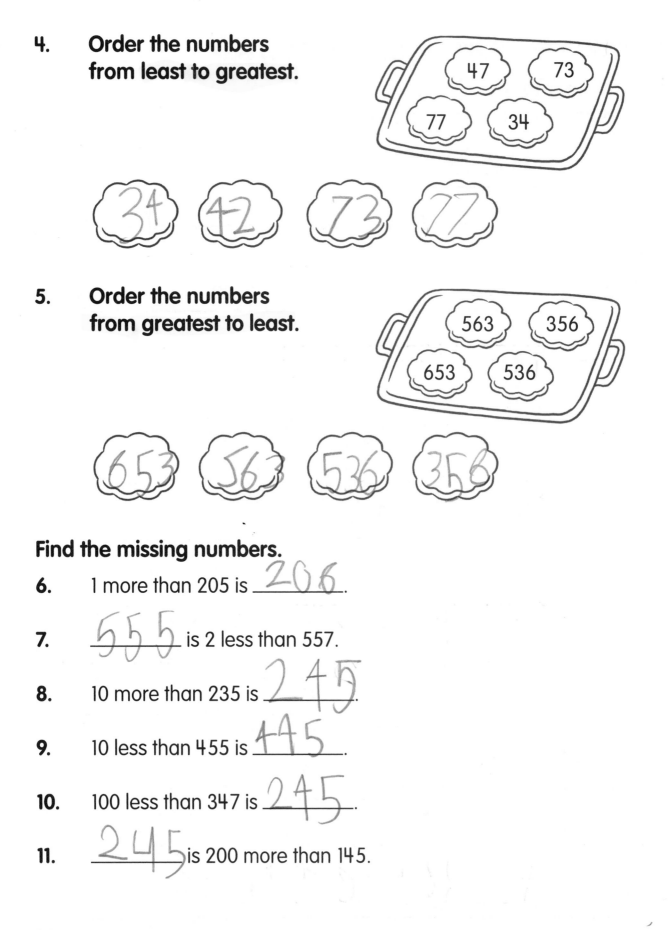

34   42   73   77

5. Order the numbers from greatest to least.

653   563   536   356

Find the missing numbers.

6. 1 more than 205 is _206_.

7. _555_ is 2 less than 557.

8. 10 more than 235 is _245_.

9. 10 less than 455 is _445_.

10. 100 less than 347 is _245_.

11. _245_ is 200 more than 145.

What is the missing number?

12.

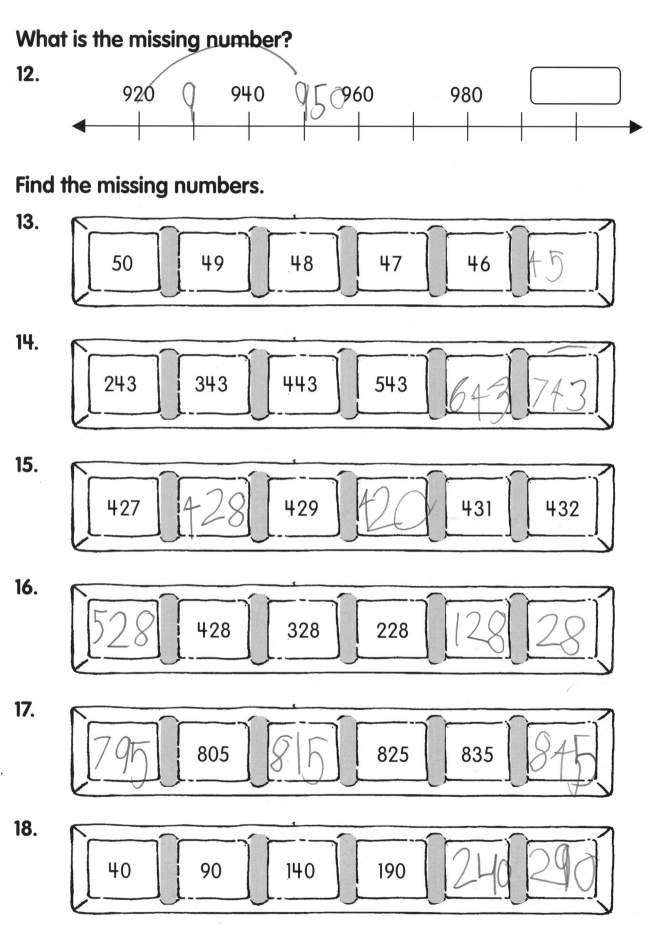

920   9   940   950 960   980   [   ]

Find the missing numbers.

13.

| 50 | 49 | 48 | 47 | 46 | 45 |

14.

| 243 | 343 | 443 | 543 | 643 | 743 |

15.

| 427 | 428 | 429 | 420 | 431 | 432 |

16.

| 528 | 428 | 328 | 228 | 128 | 28 |

17.

| 795 | 805 | 815 | 825 | 835 | 845 |

18.

| 40 | 90 | 140 | 190 | 240 | 290 |

Math Journal

Count on or count back.

1.

Every 10 counts of 1 one makes 10.

+ 1

| 132 | | | | | | | | | | |

_____ is 10 more than 132.

2.

Every _____ counts of 1 ten makes _____.

+ 10

| | | | | | | | | | | |

_____ is 100 more than _____.

Put On Your Thinking Cap!

Challenging Practice

Answer the question.

Sunny Snake has swallowed some eggs.
The eggs have numbers that follow a pattern.
Find the missing numbers.

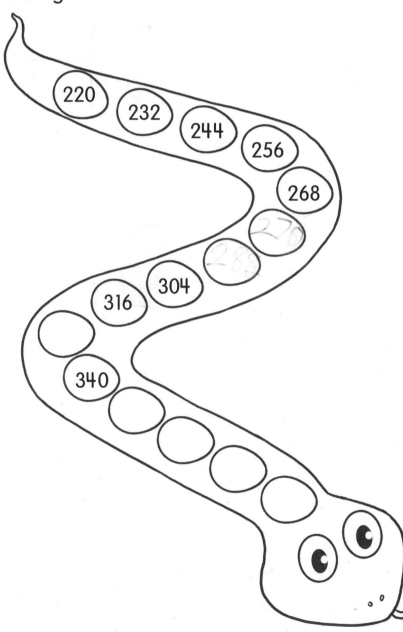

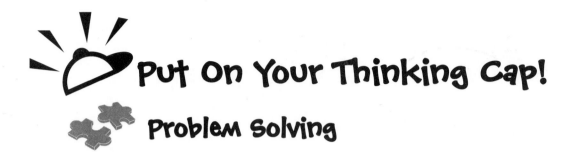

Put On Your Thinking Cap!

Problem Solving

Answer the question.

Sally and Hans started counting at the same time.
Sally counted on by tens from 300.
Hans counted back by hundreds.
After six counts, they had reached the same number.
What number did Hans start counting from?

Draw a diagram or act it out.

Chapter Review/Test

Vocabulary

1. **Match.**

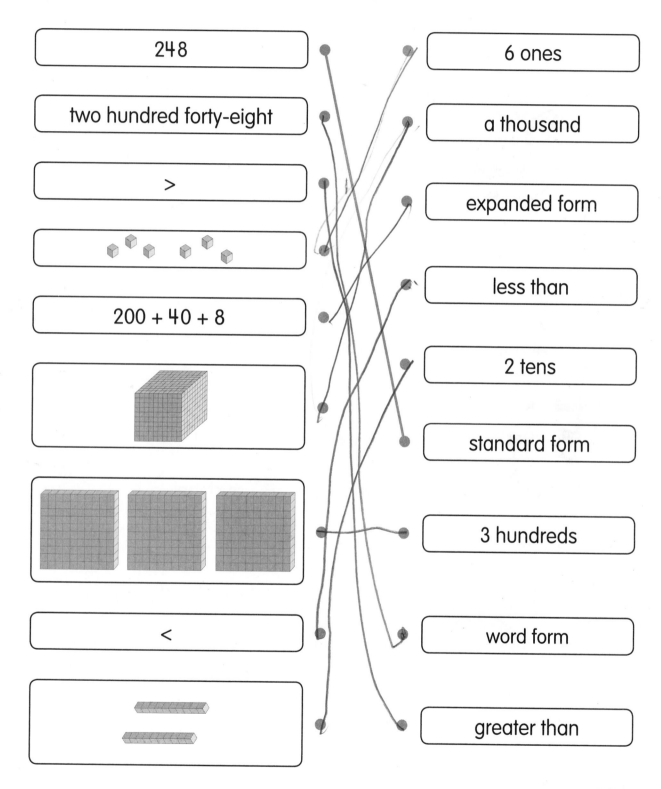

248	6 ones
two hundred forty-eight	a thousand
>	expanded form
(unit cubes)	less than
200 + 40 + 8	2 tens
(thousand cube)	standard form
(hundred flats)	3 hundreds
<	word form
(tens rods)	greater than

Concepts and Skills

Fill in the blank.

2.

Hundreds	Tens	Ones
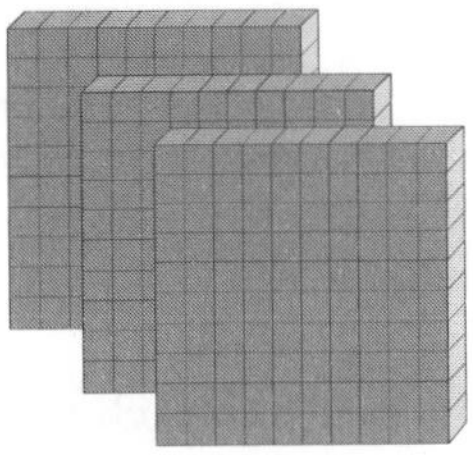	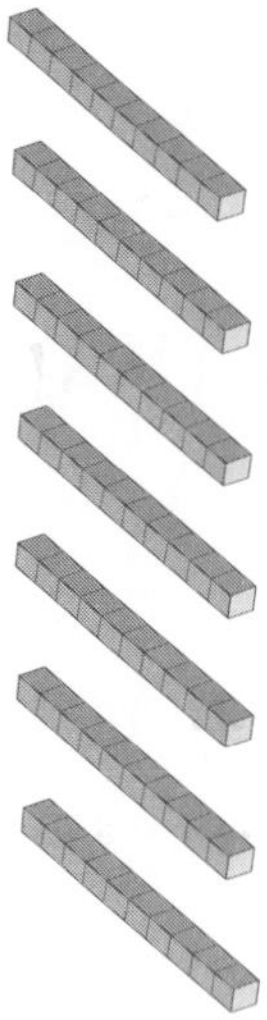	

The number shown above is __374__.

Fill in the blanks.

3. Five hundred forty-nine is the ___W___ form of 549.

4. The standard form of 549 is __549__ and the

   expanded form is __500 + 40 + 9__.

5. In 549, the digit 4 is in the __ten__ place, the digit __5__ is in

   the hundreds place, and the digit 9 is in the __ones__ place.

Name: _____   Date: _____

Fill in the missing numbers or words.

6	3	8

6. The digit 6 is in the ____H____ place,

the digit 3 is in the ____T____ place,

and the digit ____8____ is in the ones place.

Fill in the blanks.
Use the items in the box to help you.

696   969   (>)   (<)

7. ____969____ is greater than ____696____.

8.   696 ___<___ 969

9.   969 ___>___ 696

Write the numbers in order from least to greatest.
10.

384	438	843	834	483	348

348 384 438 483 834 843

Find the missing numbers.

11.   977 _967_ 957 947 _937_ _927_ 917

Problem Solving

Solve.

12. Taisha has 654 stickers.
Jan has 564 stickers and Pedro has 645 stickers.
Who has the most stickers and who has the least stickers?

_____ has the most stickers and _____ has the least stickers.

13. Winston climbed some steps.
With each step he took, he counted on by tens.
He started counting from the number 50 (Step 1)
and stopped when he counted to 120.

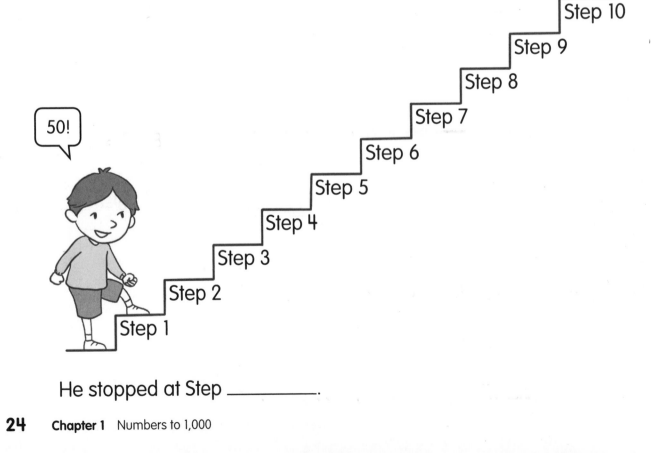

He stopped at Step _____.

Name: _____   Date: _____

 **CHAPTER**

2 Addition up to 1,000

Practice 1   Addition and Subtraction Facts Within 20

Find the missing numbers.
Add mentally.

Example

7 + 6 = ?

6 = __3__ + __3__

7 + __3__ = __10__

So, 7 + 6 = __10__ + __3__

      = __13__

1.   5 + 9 = _____

2.   8 + 9 = _____

3.   9 + 6 = _____

4.   9 + 9 = _____

Example

7 + 6 = ?

7 = __6__ + __1__

__6__ + __6__ = __12__

So, 6 + 7 = __6__ + __6__ + __1__

      = __12__ + __1__

      = __13__

5.   8 + 7 = _____

6.   8 + 6 = _____

7.   9 + 3 = _____

8.   9 + 7 = _____

9.   9 + 9 = _____

Subtract mentally.

Example

12 − 3 = ?

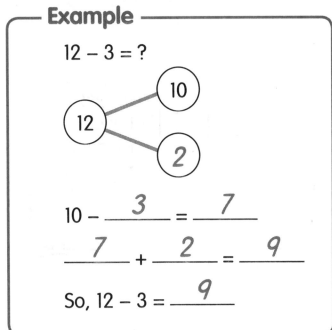

10 − __3__ = __7__

__7__ + __2__ = __9__

So, 12 − 3 = __9__

10.   16 − 9 = ?

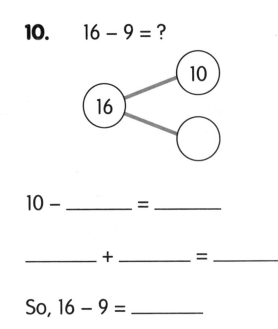

10 − _____ = _____

_____ + _____ = _____

So, 16 − 9 = _____

Subtract mentally.

11.   13 − 8 = _____

12.   11 − 6 = _____

13.   15 − 7 = _____

14.   14 − 8 = _____

15.   13 − 5 = _____

16.   17 − 9 = _____

Practice 2   Addition Without Regrouping

Add.

1.   232 + 645 = ?

Add the ones.
2 ones + 5 ones = ____7____ ones

Add the tens.
3 tens + 4 tens = ____7____ tens

Add the hundreds.
2 hundreds + 6 hundreds = ____8____ hundreds

232 + 645 = __877__

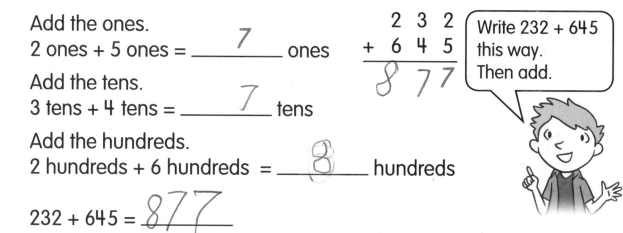

$$\begin{array}{r} 2\ 3\ 2 \\ +\ 6\ 4\ 5 \\ \hline 8\ 7\ 7 \end{array}$$

Write 232 + 645 this way. Then add.

2.
$$\begin{array}{r} 1\ 0\ 8 \\ +\ \ 8\ 7\ 1 \\ \hline 9\ 7\ 9 \end{array}$$

3.
$$\begin{array}{r} 7\ 9 \\ +\ 8\ 2\ 0 \\ \hline 8\ 9\ 9 \end{array}$$

4.   122 + 473 = __595__

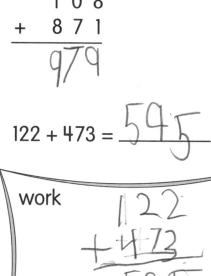

work

$$\begin{array}{r} 1\ 2\ 2 \\ +\ 4\ 7\ 3 \\ \hline 5\ 9\ 5 \end{array}$$

5.   217 + 771 = __988__

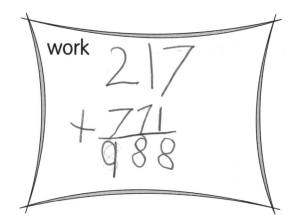

work

$$\begin{array}{r} 2\ 1\ 7 \\ +\ 7\ 7\ 1 \\ \hline 9\ 8\ 8 \end{array}$$

Add.

6. Three friends have some addition cards.
Some answers will win prizes.
Help them add to find their prizes.

I win the _____.

3 4 8	0 0 3	1 3 2
+ 2 5 1	+ 2 5 1	+ 3 6
599	254	166

I win the _____.

1 7	5 5 2	3 1 3
+ 2 4 0	+ 3 4 6	+ 3 2 0
257	810	633

I win the _____.

7 6 5	5 4 3	6 5 1
+ 2 3 4	+ 3 3 3	+ 3 3
999	876	684

bears	ball	book	hat	toy car
168	989	633	876	252

Practice 3   Addition Without Regrouping

Solve.

Example

A bakery sells 567 bagels on Monday.
It sells 412 bagels on Tuesday.
How many bagels does the bakery sell on both days?

$$567 + 412 = 979$$

$$\begin{array}{r} 5\ 6\ 7 \\ +\ 4\ 1\ 2 \\ \hline 9\ 7\ 9 \end{array}$$

The bakery sells ___979___ bagels on both days.

---

1. There are 623 steps in Castle A.
   There are 245 more steps in Castle B than in Castle A.
   How many steps are there in Castle B?

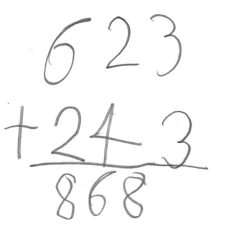

$$\begin{array}{r} 6\ 2\ 3 \\ +\ 2\ 4\ 3 \\ \hline 8\ 6\ 8 \end{array}$$

There are ___868___ steps in Castle B.

Solve.

2. Chef Lila baked 271 muffins on Saturday.
She baked another 308 muffins on Sunday.
How many muffins did Chef Lila bake in all?

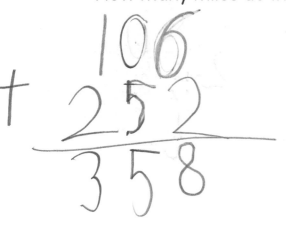

$$
\begin{array}{r}
271 \\
+\ 308 \\
\hline
579
\end{array}
$$

Chef Lila baked __579__ muffins in all.

3. The Jones family drive 106 miles on Monday.
On Tuesday they drive another 252 miles.
How many miles do they drive altogether?

$$
\begin{array}{r}
106 \\
+\ 252 \\
\hline
358
\end{array}
$$

They drive __358__ miles altogether.

Name: _____   Date: _____

4. Allen is training for a skipping contest.
He skips 373 times in the morning.
He skips 324 times in the evening.
How many times does Allen skip altogether?

$$
\begin{array}{r}
373 \\
+\ 324 \\
\hline
697 \\
\end{array}
$$

Allen skips __697__ times altogether.

5. Ladonna sold 210 tickets yesterday.
She sells 365 more tickets today than yesterday.
How many tickets does Ladonna sell today?

$$
\begin{array}{r}
210 \\
+\ 365 \\
\hline
575 \\
\end{array}
$$

Ladonna sells __575__ tickets today.

Solve.

6. Anna scores 93 points in a computer game.
    Lee scores 106 points in a computer game.
    How many points do they score altogether?

$$93$$
$$+ 106$$

They score _____ points altogether.

7. Greenwood School has 322 students.
    Seaview Preschool has 75 students.
    How many students do the schools have in all?

The schools have _____ students in all.

Practice 4   Addition with Regrouping in Ones

Add and regroup the ones.

1.   778 + 119 = ?

Add and regroup the ones.

8 ones + 9 ones = ___17___ ones

= ___1___ ten ___7___ ones

$$\begin{array}{r} {}^{\,1}7\;7\;8 \\ +\;\;1\;1\;9 \\ \hline 8\;9\;7 \end{array}$$

> Write 778 + 119 this way. Then add.

Add the tens.
1 ten + 7 tens + 1 ten = ___9___ tens

Add the hundreds.
7 hundreds + 1 hundred = ___8___ hundreds

778 + 119 = ___897___

2.
$$\begin{array}{r} 5\;|6\;|8 \\ +\;1\;|2\;|3 \\ \hline 6\;9\;1 \end{array}$$

3.
$$\begin{array}{r} 6\;|3\;|8 \\ +\;1\;|5\;|5 \\ \hline 7\;9\;3 \end{array}$$

4.   576 + 207 = ___783___

5.   631 + 329 = ___960___

work
$$\begin{array}{r} 5\;7\;6 \\ +\;2\;0\;7 \\ \hline 7\;8\;3 \end{array}$$

work
$$\begin{array}{r} 6\;3\;1 \\ +\;3\;2\;9 \\ \hline 9\;6\;0 \end{array}$$

Add.
An example is shown.

6.

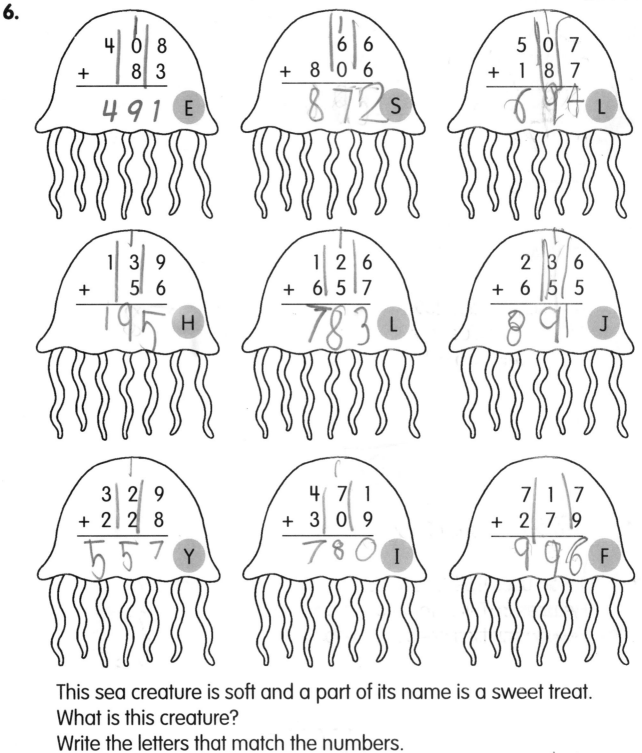

$$\begin{array}{r} 4\ 0\ 8 \\ +\ \ 8\ 3 \\ \hline 4\ 9\ 1 \end{array}$$ **E**

$$\begin{array}{r} 6\ 6 \\ +\ 8\ 0\ 6 \\ \hline 8\ 7\ 2 \end{array}$$ **S**

$$\begin{array}{r} 5\ 0\ 7 \\ +\ 1\ 8\ 7 \\ \hline 6\ 9\ 4 \end{array}$$ **L**

$$\begin{array}{r} 1\ 3\ 9 \\ +\ \ 5\ 6 \\ \hline 1\ 9\ 5 \end{array}$$ **H**

$$\begin{array}{r} 1\ 2\ 6 \\ +\ 6\ 5\ 7 \\ \hline 7\ 8\ 3 \end{array}$$ **L**

$$\begin{array}{r} 2\ 3\ 6 \\ +\ 6\ 5\ 5 \\ \hline 8\ 9\ 1 \end{array}$$ **J**

$$\begin{array}{r} 3\ 2\ 9 \\ +\ 2\ 2\ 8 \\ \hline 5\ 5\ 7 \end{array}$$ **Y**

$$\begin{array}{r} 4\ 7\ 1 \\ +\ 3\ 0\ 9 \\ \hline 7\ 8\ 0 \end{array}$$ **I**

$$\begin{array}{r} 7\ 1\ 7 \\ +\ 2\ 7\ 9 \\ \hline 9\ 9\ 6 \end{array}$$ **F**

This sea creature is soft and a part of its name is a sweet treat.
What is this creature?
Write the letters that match the numbers.

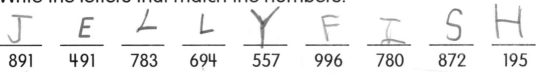

J	E	L	L	Y	F	I	S	H
891	491	783	694	557	996	780	872	195

Practice 5   Addition with Regrouping in Ones

Solve.

1. Chef Andrew makes 447 chicken sandwiches.
    He makes 46 turkey sandwiches.
    How many sandwiches does Chef Andrew make in all?

    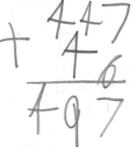

    $$\begin{array}{r} 447 \\ +\ 46 \\ \hline 497 \end{array}$$

    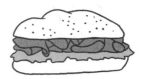

    Chef Andrew makes ___497___ sandwiches in all.

2. At a school fair, 209 cups of cider are sold in the morning.
    179 cups of cider are sold in the afternoon.
    How many cups of cider are sold?

    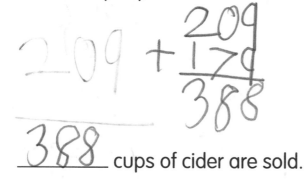

    $$209 + \begin{array}{r} 209 \\ 179 \\ \hline 388 \end{array}$$

    ___388___ cups of cider are sold.

3. Julian uses 454 tiles to cover the floor of one bedroom.
    He uses 307 tiles for another bedroom.
    How many tiles does he use for both rooms?

    $$454 + \begin{array}{r} 454 \\ 307 \\ \hline 761 \end{array}$$

    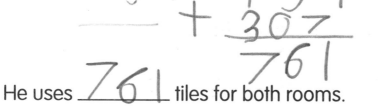

    He uses ___761___ tiles for both rooms.

Solve.

4.　Mr. Souza has 182 stamps.
His brother gives him another 209 stamps.
How many stamps does Mr. Souza have altogether?

Mr. Souza has ＿＿＿＿＿ stamps altogether.

5.　Dena decorates a patio with a string of 354 party lights.
Eric has a string of lights that has 27 more lights than
Dena's string of lights.
How many lights does Eric's string of lights have?

Eric's string of lights has ＿＿＿＿＿ lights.

6.　Lucy ties 136 red ribbons for the parade.
She ties 59 more yellow ribbons than red ribbons.
How many yellow ribbons does Lucy tie?

Lucy ties ＿＿＿＿＿ yellow ribbons.

Practice 6   Addition with Regrouping in Tens

Add and regroup the tens.

1.   534 + 283 = ?

   Add the ones.

   4 ones + 3 ones = _____ ones

   Add and regroup the tens.

   3 tens + 8 tens = _____ tens

              = _____ hundred _____ ten

   Add the hundreds.

   1 hundred + 5 hundreds + 2 hundreds = _____ hundreds

   534 + 283 = _____

> Write 534 + 283
> this way.
>
>   5   3   4
> + 2   8   3
> ———————
> Then add.

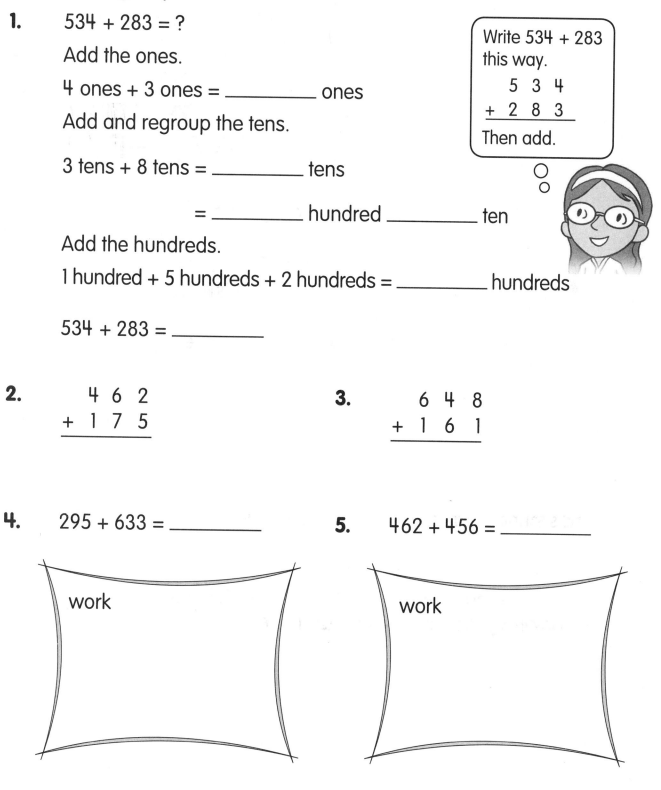

2.   4   6   2
   + 1   7   5
   ———————

3.   6   4   8
   + 1   6   1
   ———————

4.   295 + 633 = _____

   work

5.   462 + 456 = _____

   work

Add.

6.

$$\begin{array}{r} 1 \\ 65 \\ +\ 652 \\ \hline 857 \end{array}$$

$$\begin{array}{r} 1 \\ 591 \\ +\ 82 \\ \hline 683 \end{array}$$

$$\begin{array}{r} 476 \\ +\ 483 \\ \hline 959 \end{array}$$

$$\begin{array}{r} 1 \\ 869 \\ +\ 50 \\ \hline 919 \end{array}$$

$$\begin{array}{r} 1 \\ 533 \\ +\ 274 \\ \hline 807 \end{array}$$

$$\begin{array}{r} 1 \\ 354 \\ +\ 194 \\ \hline 548 \end{array}$$

$$\begin{array}{r} 1 \\ 97 \\ +\ 820 \\ \hline 917 \end{array}$$

$$\begin{array}{r} 1 \\ 426 \\ +\ 381 \\ \hline 807 \end{array}$$

Kim lost her robots.
Her robots have the same answer.
To help her find her robots, color the robots with the same answer.

Practice 7 Addition with Regrouping in Tens

Solve.

1. Farmer Black has 374 chickens and 383 ducks on his farm.
    How many ducks and chickens does he have in all?

    $$\begin{array}{r} 38 \\ +\ 3\ 2 \\ \hline \end{array}$$

    He has _____ ducks and chickens in all.

2. Maria has 381 baseball cards.
    She has 492 football cards.
    How many cards does she have in all?

    She has _____ cards in all.

3. Peter collects 280 stamps.
    Then his brother gives him another 163 stamps.
    How many stamps does Peter have now?

    Peter has _____ stamps now.

Solve.

4. Kirk has painted 460 bricks.
He has 262 bricks left to paint.
How many bricks does Kirk have to paint in all?

Kirk has to paint _____ bricks in all.

5. Leroy has 299 model airplanes.
Keisha gives him another 120 model airplanes.
How many model airplanes does Leroy have now?

Leroy has _____ model airplanes now.

6. A parking garage has 654 vans.
It has 191 more cars than vans.
How many cars are in the garage?

_____ cars are in the garage.

© Marshall Cavendish International (Singapore) Private Limited.

Practice 8 Addition with Regrouping in Ones and Tens

Add and regroup.

1. 488 + 123 = ?

    Add and regroup the ones.
    8 ones + 3 ones

    = _____ ones

    = _____ ten _____ one

    Add and regroup the tens.

    1 ten + 8 tens + 2 tens = _____ tens

    = _____ hundred _____ ten

    Add the hundreds.

    1 hundred + 4 hundreds + 1 hundred = _____ hundreds

    488 + 123 = _____

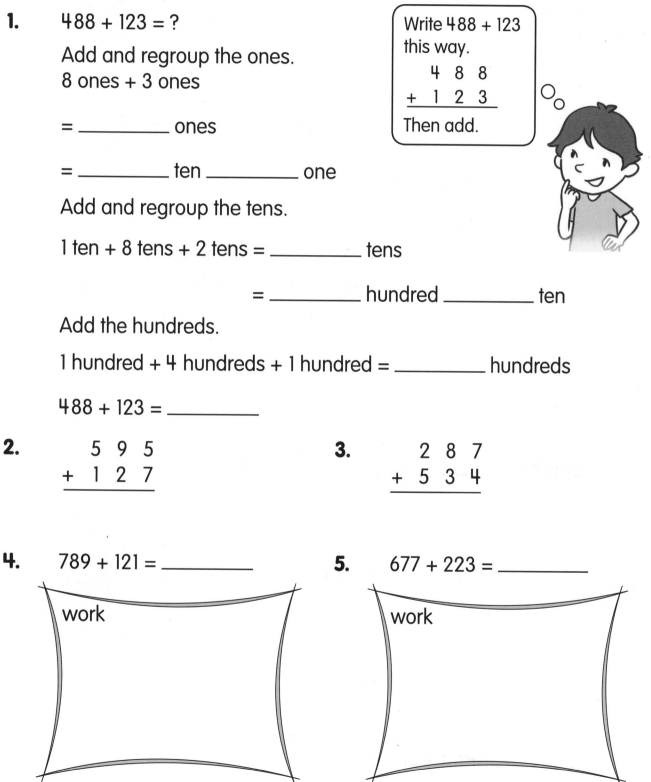

Write 488 + 123
this way.
```
  4 8 8
+ 1 2 3
```
Then add.

2.
```
  5 9 5
+ 1 2 7
```

3.
```
  2 8 7
+ 5 3 4
```

4. 789 + 121 = _____

    work

5. 677 + 223 = _____

    work

Whose toys are these?
Add.
Then match the owner to the toy.

6.

$$
\begin{array}{r}
\overset{1}{}\overset{1}{}5\ 6 \\
+\ 2\ 5\ 7 \\
\hline
3\ 1\ 3
\end{array}
$$

700

298

$$
\begin{array}{r}
\overset{1}{}\overset{1}{}9\ 9 \\
+\quad\ 9\ 9 \\
\hline
2\ 9\ 8
\end{array}
$$

313

$$
\begin{array}{r}
\overset{1}{}\overset{1}{}8\ 9\ 5 \\
+\quad\ 2\ 8 \\
\hline
9\ 2\ 3
\end{array}
$$

712

$$
\begin{array}{r}
\overset{1}{}\overset{1}{}4\ 0\ 3 \\
+\ 2\ 9\ 7 \\
\hline
7\ 0\ 0
\end{array}
$$

923

$$
\begin{array}{r}
\overset{1}{}\overset{1}{}2\ 4\ 5 \\
+\ 4\ 6\ 7 \\
\hline
7\ 1\ 2
\end{array}
$$

721

$$
\begin{array}{r}
\overset{1}{}\overset{1}{}4\ 8\ 8 \\
+\ 2\ 3\ 3 \\
\hline
7\ 2\ 1
\end{array}
$$

Practice 9 Addition with Regrouping in Ones and Tens

Solve.

1. On Wednesday, 487 people visit the zoo.
On Thursday, 135 more people visit the zoo than on Wednesday.
How many people visit the zoo on Thursday?

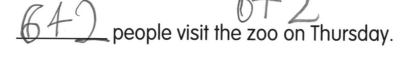

$$
\begin{array}{r}
4\,8\,7 \\
+\ 1\,3\,5 \\
\hline
6\,4\,2
\end{array}
$$

_642_ people visit the zoo on Thursday.

2. After selling 694 books, Mr. Brown has 276 books left.
How many books did he have at first?

$$
\begin{array}{r}
6\,9\,4 \\
+\ 2\,7\,6 \\
\hline
9\,7\,0
\end{array}
$$

He had _970_ books at first.

3. A toy company gives away 777 toys in a contest.
There are 177 toys left.
How many toys are there at first?

$$
\begin{array}{r}
7\,7\,7 \\
+\ 1\,7\,7 \\
\hline
9\,5\,4
\end{array}
$$

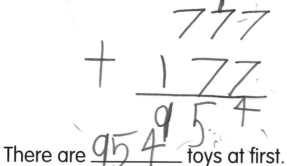

There are _954_ toys at first.

Solve.

4. There are 167 dolls in a toy store.
The owner buys 533 more dolls.
How many dolls are there now?

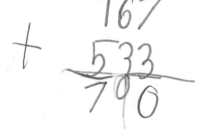

$$\begin{array}{r} 167 \\ +\ 533 \\ \hline 790 \end{array}$$

There are ___700___ dolls now.

5. Sunshine Camp has 324 boys.
There are 379 girls.
How many campers are at Sunshine Camp?

$$\begin{array}{r} 324 \\ +\ 379 \\ \hline 703 \end{array}$$

There are ___703___ campers at Sunshine Camp.

6. Luke has 548 coins in his collection.
Luke has 276 fewer coins than Sam.
How many coins does Sam have?

$$\begin{array}{r} 548 \\ +\ 276 \\ \hline 824 \end{array}$$

Sam has ___824___ coins in his collection.

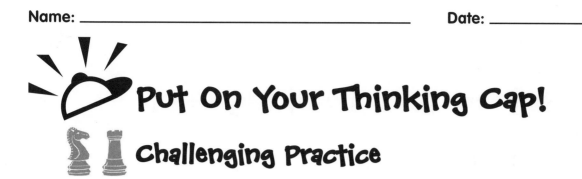

Put On Your Thinking Cap!

Challenging Practice

Write the missing numbers.

1.

```
    5 3 ☐
  +  1 4 1
  ———————
    6 7 4
```

2.

```
    ☐ 4 5
  +  2 3 4
  ———————
    8 7 9
```

3.

```
    7 ☐ 8
  +  2 9 1
  ———————
    9 9 9
```

4.

```
    4 2 6
  +  3 ☐ 5
  ———————
    7 6 1
```

5.

```
    3 ☐ 7
  +  5 9 5
  ———————
    9 3 2
```

6.

```
    6 5 3
  +  2 ☐ 9
  ———————
    9 4 2
```

Do these.

7.

(455) (544) (554) (545) (454)

a. Order the numbers from greatest to least.

b. Add 100 to the least number.
Show your work.

Put On Your Thinking Cap!

Problem Solving

Make two 3-digit numbers from the numbers below.
Use each number only once.
What are the two 3-digit numbers that give the greatest
answer when you add them?

| 3 | 5 | 2 | 4 | 1 | 0 |

_____   _____   _____

Chapter Review/Test

Vocabulary

Fill in the blanks with words from the box.
The words may be used more than once.

1.

ones	tens	hundreds	regroup	hundred

```
    1
  4 6 2
+ 2 6 8
───────
      0
```

Step 1

Add the _ones_.

Use basic facts.

2 + 8 = 10

2 ones + 8 ones = 10 ones

regroup the ones.

10 ones = 1 ten 0 ones

```
  1 1
  4 6 2
+ 2 6 8
───────
    3 0
```

Step 2

Add the _tens_.

Use double facts.

1 + 6 + 6 = 13

1 ten + 6 tens + 6 tens = 13 tens

regroup the tens.

13 tens = 1 _hundreds_ 3 _tens_

130

```
  1 1
  4 6 2
+ 2 6 8
───────
  7 3 0
```

Step 3

Add the _hundreds_.

1 hundred + 4 hundreds + 2 hundreds

= 7 hundreds

462 + 268 = 730

Concepts and Skills

Add.
Then match the problems with the same answer.

2.

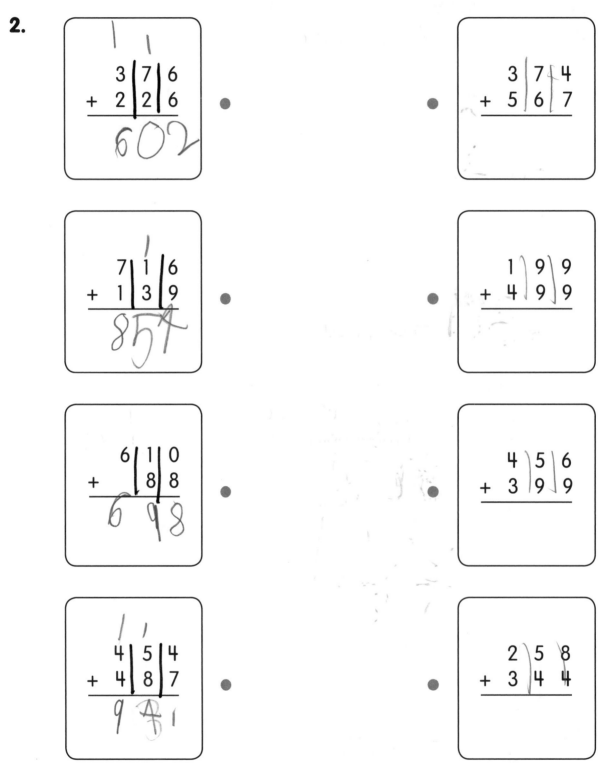

$$\begin{array}{r} \overset{1}{3}\,\overset{1}{7}\,6 \\ +\ 2\,2\,6 \\ \hline 602 \end{array}$$

$$\begin{array}{r} 3\,7\,4 \\ +\ 5\,6\,7 \\ \hline \end{array}$$

$$\begin{array}{r} 7\,\overset{1}{1}\,6 \\ +\ 1\,3\,9 \\ \hline 857 \end{array}$$

$$\begin{array}{r} 1\,9\,9 \\ +\ 4\,9\,9 \\ \hline \end{array}$$

$$\begin{array}{r} 6\,1\,0 \\ +\ \ \ 8\,8 \\ \hline 698 \end{array}$$

$$\begin{array}{r} 4\,5\,6 \\ +\ 3\,9\,9 \\ \hline \end{array}$$

$$\begin{array}{r} \overset{1}{4}\,\overset{1}{5}\,4 \\ +\ 4\,8\,7 \\ \hline 941 \end{array}$$

$$\begin{array}{r} 2\,5\,8 \\ +\ 3\,4\,4 \\ \hline \end{array}$$

Problem Solving

Solve.

3.   Mr. Thomas drives 173 miles on Monday.
On Tuesday, he drives 216 miles.
How many miles does he drive in all?

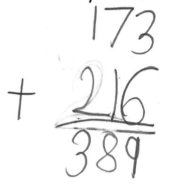

$$
\begin{array}{r}
173 \\
+\ 216 \\
\hline
389
\end{array}
$$

He drives ___389___ miles in all.

4.   A carpenter has 362 pieces of lumber.
He needs another 228 pieces of lumber to build a bridge.
How many pieces of lumber does he need to build the bridge?

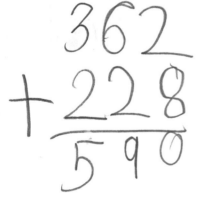

$$
\begin{array}{r}
362 \\
+\ 228 \\
\hline
590
\end{array}
$$

He needs ___590___ pieces of lumber to build the bridge.

Solve.

5. A movie theater sells 294 tickets to the first show.
It sells 457 tickets to the second show.
How many tickets does it sell in all?

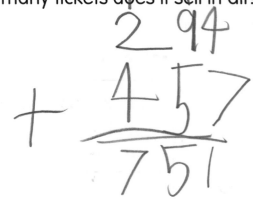

It sells _751_ tickets in all.

6. Shantel has 546 stickers in her collection.
She has 278 fewer stickers than Sherice.
How many stickers does Sherice have in her collection?

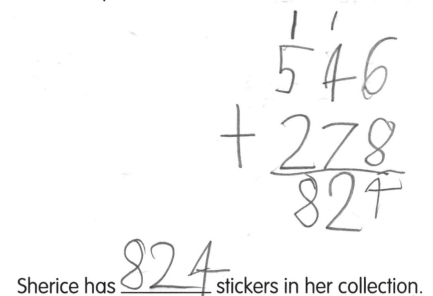

Sherice has _824_ stickers in her collection.

CHAPTER 3 Subtraction up to 1,000

Practice 1   Subtraction Without Regrouping

Subtract.

1.   432 − 221 = ?

Subtract the ones.
2 ones − 1 one = __1__ one

Subtract the tens.
3 tens − 2 tens = __1__ ten

Subtract the hundreds.
4 hundreds − 2 hundreds = __2__ hundreds

432 − 221 = __211__

Use addition to check your answer.

> Write 432 − 221 this way.
>   4 3 2
> −   2 2 1
> ―――――――
>   211
> Then subtract.

        211
    + 2 2 1
   ――――――――
      4 3 2

2.   6 8 5   3.   5 6 6   4.   7 9 7
    −   7 1   −   4 1 3   −   5 2 7
   ―――――――――   ―――――――――   ―――――――――
      6 1 4   1 5 3   2 7 0

5.   999 − 693 = __306__   6.   864 − 354 = __510__

work 999   306   work 864   510
    − 693   + 693   − 354   + 354
   ―――――   ―――――   ―――――   ―――――
    306   999   510   864

Subtract.

Example

$$572 - 262 = ?$$

$$
\begin{array}{r}
572 \\
-\ 262 \\
\hline
310
\end{array}
$$

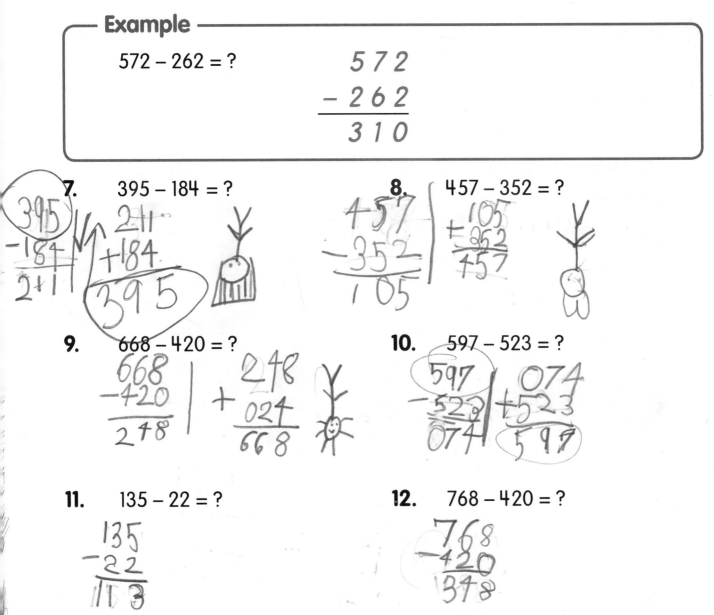

7. $395 - 184 = ?$

$$
\begin{array}{r}
395 \\
-184 \\
\hline
211
\end{array}
$$

$$
\begin{array}{r}
211 \\
+184 \\
\hline
395
\end{array}
$$

8. $457 - 352 = ?$

$$
\begin{array}{r}
457 \\
-352 \\
\hline
105
\end{array}
$$

$$
\begin{array}{r}
105 \\
+352 \\
\hline
457
\end{array}
$$

9. $668 - 420 = ?$

$$
\begin{array}{r}
668 \\
-420 \\
\hline
248
\end{array}
$$

$$
\begin{array}{r}
248 \\
+024 \\
\hline
668
\end{array}
$$

10. $597 - 523 = ?$

$$
\begin{array}{r}
597 \\
-523 \\
\hline
074
\end{array}
$$

$$
\begin{array}{r}
074 \\
+523 \\
\hline
597
\end{array}
$$

11. $135 - 22 = ?$

$$
\begin{array}{r}
135 \\
-\ 22 \\
\hline
113
\end{array}
$$

12. $768 - 420 = ?$

$$
\begin{array}{r}
768 \\
-420 \\
\hline
348
\end{array}
$$

Look for the answers in the puzzle and circle them.
They can only be in the direction ↓, →, or ↘.
Your answers may overlap.

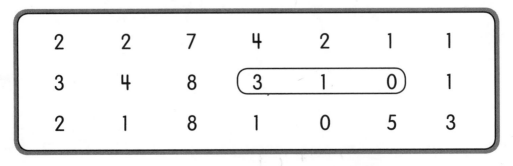

2	2	7	4	2	1	1
3	4	8	3	1	0	1
2	1	8	1	0	5	3

Practice 2   Subtraction Without Regrouping

Solve.
Show how to check your answer.

Example

Mr. Ong's orchard has 175 trees.
152 trees grow fruit.
How many trees do not grow fruit?

$$175 - 152 = 23$$

$$\begin{array}{r} 1\,7\,5 \\ -\ 1\,5\,2 \\ \hline 2\,3 \end{array}$$

_____23_____ trees do not grow fruit.

---

1.   Gina has 436 beads.
     She uses 123 beads to make a necklace.
     How many beads does she have left?

     She has ___313___ beads left.

2.   David's book has 345 pages.
     He reads 231 pages of the book.
     How many pages does he have left to read?

$$\begin{array}{r} 3\,4\,5 \\ -\ 2\,3\,1 \\ \hline 2\,1\,4 \end{array}$$

$$\begin{array}{r} 2\,1\,4 \\ +\ 2\,3\,1 \\ \hline 4\,4\,5 \end{array}$$

     He has ___214___ pages left to read.

Solve.
Show how to check your answer.

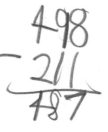

$$\begin{array}{r} 498 \\ -\ 211 \\ \hline 487 \end{array}$$

3. The lunchroom has 498 chairs.
The janitor removes 211 chairs.
How many chairs are left in the lunchroom?

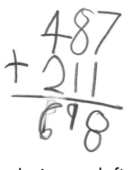

$$\begin{array}{r} 487 \\ +\ 211 \\ \hline 698 \end{array}$$

_487_ chairs are left in the lunchroom.

4. Last year, Kennedy School recycled 745 plastic bottles.
This year, the school recycled 133 fewer plastic bottles than last year.
How many plastic bottles did the school recycle this year?

$$\begin{array}{r} 612 \\ +\ 133 \\ \hline 745 \end{array}$$

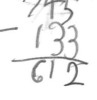

$$\begin{array}{r} 745 \\ -\ 133 \\ \hline 612 \end{array}$$

Kennedy School recycled _612_ plastic bottles this year.

5. A pilot made 347 flights last year.
He made 124 fewer flights this year than last year.
How many flights did the pilot make this year?

$$\begin{array}{r} 347 \\ +\ 124 \\ \hline 463 \end{array}$$

The pilot made _____ flights this year.

Practice 3   Subtraction with Regrouping in Tens and Ones

**Regroup the tens and ones.
Then subtract.**

Write 242 – 117 this way.

$$\begin{array}{r} 2\ \cancel{4}\ \cancel{2}{}^{3\,12} \\ -\ 1\ 1\ 7 \\ \hline 5\ 2\ 5 \end{array}$$

Then subtract.

1.   242 – 117 = ?

242 – 117

= 2 hundreds 4 tens 2 ones – 1 hundred
   1 ten 7 ones

= 2 hundreds 3 tens __12__ ones
   – 1 hundred 1 ten 7 ones

= __1__ hundred __2__ tens __5__ ones

= __125__

242 – 117 = __125__

Use addition to check your answer.

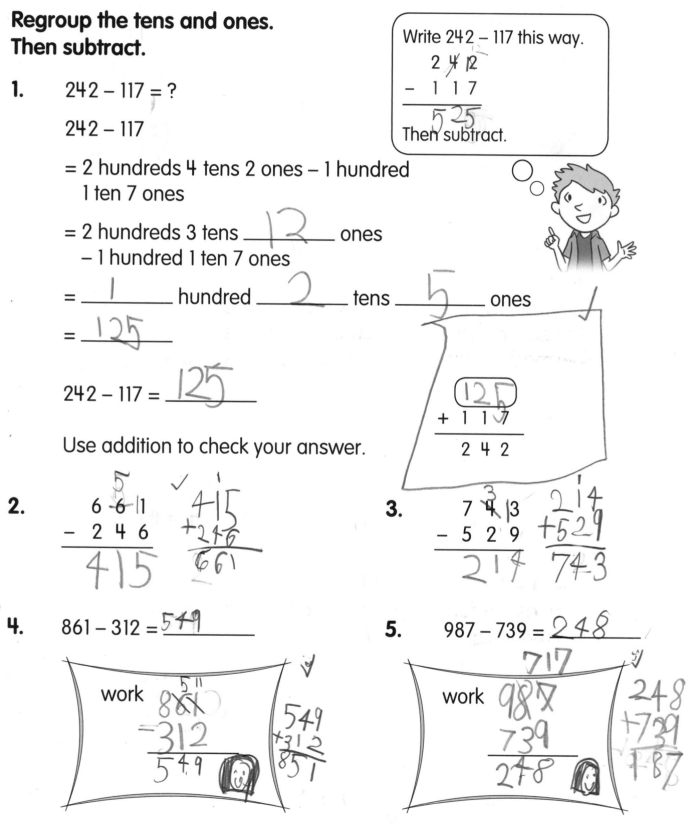

$$\boxed{125} \\ +\ 1\ 1\ 7 \\ \hline 2\ 4\ 2$$

2.
$$\begin{array}{r} {}^{5}\ 6\ \cancel{6}\ 11 \\ -\ 2\ 4\ 6 \\ \hline 4\ 1\ 5 \end{array} \qquad \begin{array}{r} 4\ 1\ 5 \\ +\ 2\ 4\ 6 \\ \hline 6\ 6\ 1 \end{array}$$

3.
$$\begin{array}{r} 7\ \cancel{4}{}^{3}\ \cancel{3}{}^{13} \\ -\ 5\ 2\ 9 \\ \hline 2\ 1\ 4 \end{array} \qquad \begin{array}{r} {}^{2\ 1}4 \\ +\ 5\ 2\ 9 \\ \hline 7\ 4\ 3 \end{array}$$

4.   861 – 312 = __549__

work
$$\begin{array}{r} {}^{5\ 11}8\,6\,\cancel{1} \\ -\ 3\ 1\ 2 \\ \hline 5\ 4\ 9 \end{array} \qquad \begin{array}{r} 5\ 4\ 9 \\ +\ 3\ 1\ 2 \\ \hline 8\ 5\ 1 \end{array}$$

5.   987 – 739 = __248__

work
$$\begin{array}{r} {}^{7\ 17}9\,8\,\cancel{7} \\ 7\ 3\ 9 \\ \hline 2\ 4\ 8 \end{array} \qquad \begin{array}{r} 2\ 4\ 8 \\ +\ 7\ 3\ 9 \\ \hline 7\ 8\ 7 \end{array}$$

6. Subtract and match.
The first one is done for you.

$$
\begin{array}{r}
3\ 5\ 4 \\
-\ 2\ 3\ 5 \\
\hline
1\ 1\ 9
\end{array}
$$

$$
\begin{array}{r}
4\ 8\ 0 \\
-\ 1\ 6\ 8 \\
\hline
3\ 1\ 2
\end{array}
$$

$$
\begin{array}{r}
5\ 5\ 5 \\
-\ 2\ 4\ 6 \\
\hline
3\ 0\ 9
\end{array}
$$

$$
\begin{array}{r}
3\ 5\ 7 \\
-\ 1\ 3\ 9 \\
\hline
2\ 1\ 8
\end{array}
$$

218

309

312

119

Practice 4   Subtraction with Regrouping in Tens and Ones

Solve.
Show how to check your answer.

$$\begin{array}{r} 1 \\ 206 \\ +058 \\ \hline 264 \end{array}$$

1.   Calvin counts 264 red toy cars at a toy shop.
     Leanne counts 58 <u>fewer</u> blue toy cars than Calvin.
     How many cars does Leanne count?

$$\begin{array}{r} 514 \\ 2\cancel{6}\cancel{4} \\ -058 \\ \hline 206 \end{array}$$

     Leanne counts __206__ cars.

2.   A library has 985 books.
     547 of them are borrowed.
     How many books are left?

$$\begin{array}{r} 715 \\ 9\cancel{8}\cancel{5} \\ -547 \\ \hline 438 \end{array}$$

$$\begin{array}{r} 4\cancel{3}7 \\ +547 \\ \hline 970 \end{array}$$

     __438__ books are left.

3.   During one week, 231 animals were brought to an animal shelter.
     112 of them were adopted.
     How many animals are still at the animal shelter?

$$\begin{array}{r} 11\cancel{2} \\ +11\cancel{9} \\ \hline 221 \end{array}$$

$$\begin{array}{r} 211 \\ 2\cancel{3}\cancel{1} \\ -112 \\ \hline 119 \end{array}$$

     __119__ animals are still at the animal shelter.

Solve.
Show how to check your answer.

4. 464 cars are parked in a parking lot.
    There are 345 fewer trucks than cars in the lot.
    How many trucks are in the parking lot?

_____ trucks are in the parking lot.

5. King Elementary School has 961 students.
    555 of the students are girls.
    How many students are boys?

_____ students are boys.

6. Cally makes 628 Chinese dumplings for the fair.
    She fries 309 of the Chinese dumplings and steams the rest.
    How many Chinese dumplings does Cally steam?

Cally steams _____ Chinese dumplings.

Practice 5   Subtraction with Regrouping in Hundreds and Tens

**Regroup the hundreds and tens.
Then subtract.**

> Write 335 – 142 this way.
>
> ```
>     3 3 5
>  –  1 4 2
>  ─────────
> ```
>
> Then subtract.

1.   335 – 142 = ?

335 – 142

= 3 hundreds 3 tens 5 ones – 1 hundred
   4 tens 2 ones

= 2 hundreds _____ tens 5 ones
   – 1 hundred 4 tens 2 ones

= _____ hundred _____ tens _____ ones

= _____

335 – 142 = _____

Use addition to check your answer.

```
    +  1 4 2
  ─────────
     3 3 5
```

2.
```
    6 6 9
  – 2 8 1
  ─────────
```

3.
```
    7 1 4
  – 3 6 3
  ─────────
```

4.   765 – 695 = _____

work

_____

5.   908 – 568 = _____

work

_____

Subtract.

6.

$$
\begin{array}{r}
3\ 4\ 8 \\
-\ 2\ 8\ 2 \\
\hline
\end{array}
$$

$$
\begin{array}{r}
4\ 0\ 9 \\
-\ 1\ 2\ 8 \\
\hline
\end{array}
$$

$$
\begin{array}{r}
2\ 3\ 9 \\
-\ \ \ 6\ 7 \\
\hline
\end{array}
$$

$$
\begin{array}{r}
4\ 1\ 3 \\
-\ 3\ 6\ 1 \\
\hline
\end{array}
$$

$$
\begin{array}{r}
5\ 5\ 5 \\
-\ 1\ 9\ 5 \\
\hline
\end{array}
$$

$$
\begin{array}{r}
6\ 3\ 8 \\
-\ 3\ 5\ 6 \\
\hline
\end{array}
$$

$$
\begin{array}{r}
8\ 1\ 9 \\
-\ \ \ 9\ 9 \\
\hline
\end{array}
$$

$$
\begin{array}{r}
7\ 1\ 9 \\
-\ 5\ 2\ 5 \\
\hline
\end{array}
$$

Practice 6 Subtraction with Regrouping in Hundreds and Tens

Solve.
Show how to check your answer.

1. A store has 519 model airplanes.
   It sells 228 model airplanes.
   How many model airplanes are left?

   There are _____ model airplanes left.

2. A florist sells 755 roses in the morning.
   She sells 191 roses in the afternoon.
   How many fewer roses does she sell in the afternoon?

   She sells _____ fewer roses in the afternoon.

3. 478 babies were born in August and September.
   190 babies were born in August.
   How many babies were born in September?

   _____ babies were born in September.

Solve.
Show how to check your answer.

4. Washington Elementary School has 883 students.
   693 of the students go to the school baseball game.
   How many students do not go to the game?

   _____ students do not go to the game.

5. 366 beads are in a box.
   195 of the beads are green.
   How many of the beads are not green?

   _____ of the beads are not green.

6. Maria has 534 kites at her shop.
   She sells 452 of the kites in a week.
   How many kites does Maria have left?

   Maria has _____ kites left.

Practice 7   Subtraction with Regrouping in Hundreds, Tens, and Ones

Regroup.
Then subtract.

1.   241 – 173 = ?

241 – 173

= 2 hundreds 4 tens 1 one – 1 hundred
  7 tens 3 ones

= 2 hundreds _____ tens 11 ones
  – 1 hundred 7 tens 3 ones

= _____ hundred 13 tens 11 ones – 1 hundred
  7 tens 3 ones

= _____ hundreds _____ tens _____ ones

= _____

241 – 173 = _____

Use addition to check your answer.

> Write 241 – 173 this way.
>
>   2 4 1
> –   1 7 3
> _____
>
> Then subtract.

```
     +  1  7  3
     _____
        2  4  1
```

2.   4 7 8
        – 1 9 9
        _____

3.   5 5 5
        – 4 5 7
        _____

4.   924 – 886 = _____

work

_____

5.   818 – 669 = _____

work

_____

**Help Daryl ride past these rocks to reach the shore.
Subtract and write the correct answer on each rock.**

6.

$$\begin{array}{r} 9\ 8\ 8 \\ -\ 7\ 9\ 9 \\ \hline \end{array}$$

$$\begin{array}{r} 4\ 8\ 3 \\ -\ 2\ 9\ 7 \\ \hline \end{array}$$

$$\begin{array}{r} 2\ 1\ 2 \\ -\ 1\ 2\ 3 \\ \hline \end{array}$$

$$\begin{array}{r} 6\ 3\ 4 \\ -\ 1\ 9\ 6 \\ \hline \end{array}$$

$$\begin{array}{r} 4\ 4\ 6 \\ -\ 2\ 6\ 8 \\ \hline \end{array}$$

$$\begin{array}{r} 6\ 6\ 1 \\ -\ 3\ 7\ 4 \\ \hline \end{array}$$

$$\begin{array}{r} 5\ 3\ 5 \\ -\ 4\ 6\ 8 \\ \hline \end{array}$$

$$\begin{array}{r} 7\ 8\ 4 \\ -\ 5\ 9\ 6 \\ \hline \end{array}$$

$$\begin{array}{r} 1\ 3\ 6 \\ -\ \ \ 9\ 9 \\ \hline \end{array}$$

$$\begin{array}{r} 8\ 8\ 3 \\ -\ 1\ 9\ 8 \\ \hline \end{array}$$

Practice 8   Subtraction with Regrouping in Hundreds, Tens, and Ones

Solve.
Show how to check your answer.

1.   817 children will march in the Thanksgiving Day Parade.
359 of the children are girls.
How many are boys?

_____ are boys.

2.   There are 605 children at a swimming pool.
There are 278 girls.
How many are boys?

_____ are boys.

3.   A sandwich shop sells 456 ham sandwiches.
It sells 298 fewer cheese sandwiches than ham sandwiches.
How many cheese sandwiches does it sell?

It sells _____ cheese sandwiches.

Solve.
Show how to check your answer.

4.   Hal drove 853 miles this year on his vacation.
       This was 154 more miles than he drove last year.
       How many miles did Hal drive on vacation last year?

       Hal drove _____ miles on vacation last year.

5.   Mrs. Ruiz makes 381 glasses of apple juice for a school fair.
       She sells 192 glasses.
       How many glasses of apple juice does Mrs. Ruiz have left?

       Mrs. Ruiz has _____ glasses of apple juice left.

6.   Tracey has 982 stickers.
       She has 496 stickers more than Zach.
       How many stickers does Zach have?

       Zach has _____ stickers.

Practice 9 Subtraction Across Zeros

Regroup.
Then subtract.

> Write 200 – 45 this way.
> ```
>   2 0 0
> –   4 5
> ```
> ─────────
> Then subtract.

1. 200 – 45 = ?

    200 = 2 hundreds

    = 1 hundred _____ tens

    = 1 hundred _____ tens 10 ones

    200 – 45 = _____

    Use addition to check your answer.

    ```
         ____
    +    4 5
    ─────────
      2 0 0
    ```

2.
```
    4 0 0
  –   9 9
─────────
```

3.
```
    5 0 0
  – 3 8 6
─────────
```

4.
```
    8 0 0
  – 7 7 9
─────────
```

5.
```
    6 0 0
  – 2 1 6
─────────
```

6. 900 – 789 = _____

7. 700 – 423 = _____

work

_____

work

_____

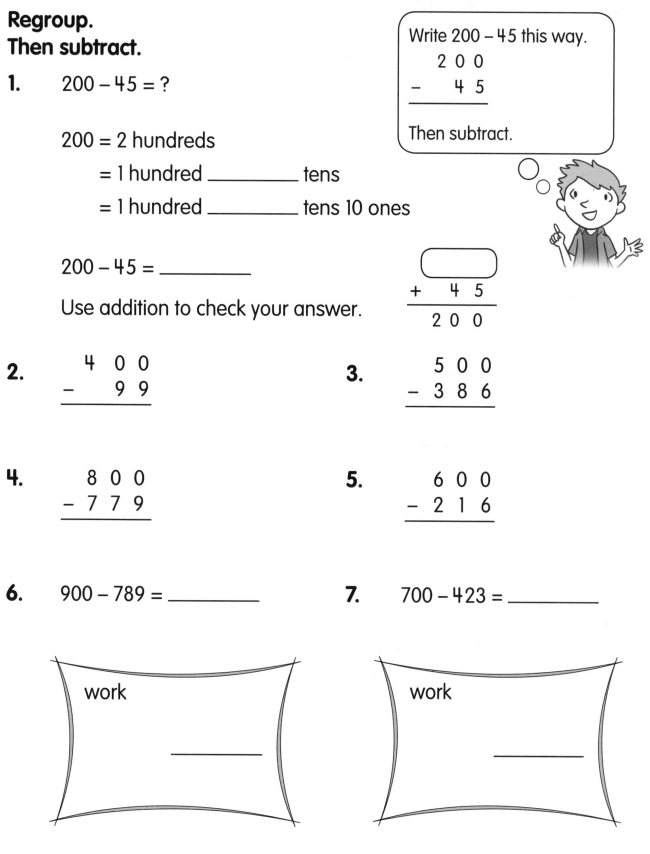

Solve.
Show how to check your answer.

8. 700 children enter an art contest.
98 of them win a prize.
How many children do not win a prize?

_____ children do not win a prize.

9. The library needs to order 600 books.
It has ordered 263 books.
How many more books does
the library still need to order?

The library still needs to order _____ more books.

10. 500 adults are at a concert.
291 of them are women.
How many men are at the concert?

There are _____ men at the concert.

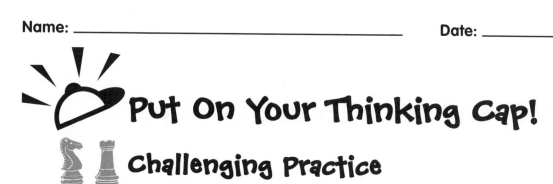

Put On Your Thinking Cap!

Challenging Practice

Write the missing numbers.

1.
```
    2 ☐ 4
 -  1 2 3
 ─────────
    1 5 1
```

2.
```
   ☐ 9 9
 - 3 2 8
 ─────────
   2 7 1
```

3.
```
    8 1 6
 -  6 ☐ 5
 ─────────
    1 9 1
```

4.
```
    5 0 0
 -  3 ☐ 4
 ─────────
    1 4 6
```

5.
```
    7 0 ☐
 -  2 5 1
 ─────────
    4 4 9
```

6.
```
    9 ☐ 3
 -  4 7 6
 ─────────
    4 2 7
```

Solve.

7.

(966)   (699)   (996)   (696)   (969)

a. Write the numbers in order from greatest to least.

b. Subtract the least number from the greatest number.
Show your work.

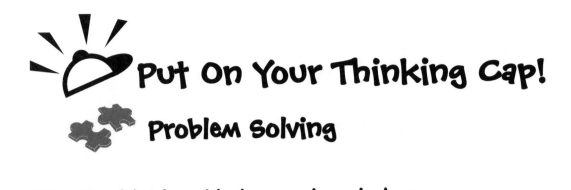

Put On Your Thinking Cap!

Problem Solving

Fill in the blanks with the numbers below.

(0)   (2)   (3)   (6)   (8)

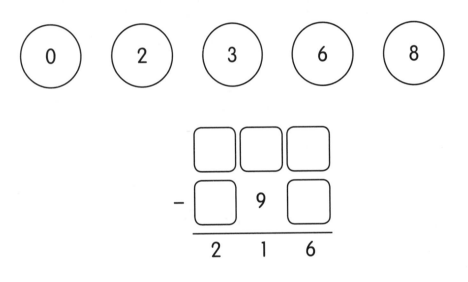

Chapter Review/Test

Vocabulary

1. **Fill in the blanks with words from the box.
    The words may be used more than once.**

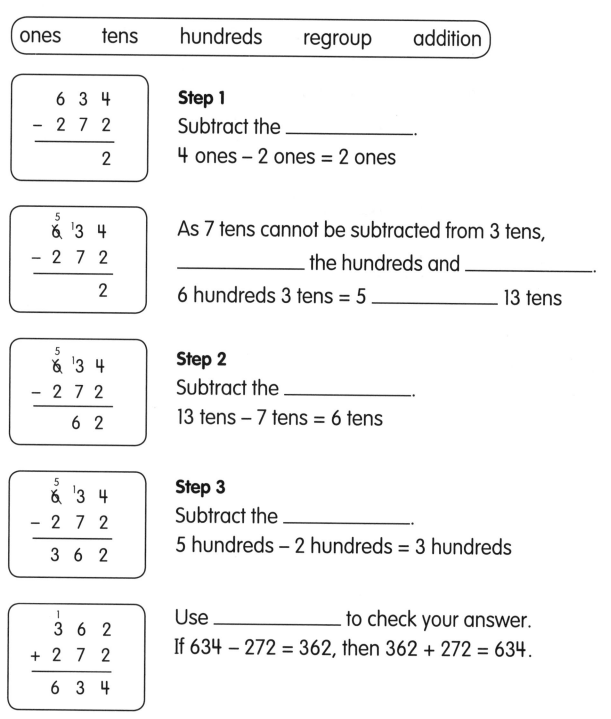

ones   tens   hundreds   regroup   addition

```
  6 3 4
- 2 7 2
-------
      2
```

Step 1
Subtract the _____.
4 ones – 2 ones = 2 ones

```
  5
  6 ¹3 4
- 2 7 2
-------
      2
```

As 7 tens cannot be subtracted from 3 tens,
_____ the hundreds and _____.
6 hundreds 3 tens = 5 _____ 13 tens

```
  5
  6 ¹3 4
- 2 7 2
-------
    6 2
```

Step 2
Subtract the _____.
13 tens – 7 tens = 6 tens

```
  5
  6 ¹3 4
- 2 7 2
-------
  3 6 2
```

Step 3
Subtract the _____.
5 hundreds – 2 hundreds = 3 hundreds

```
  1
  3 6 2
+ 2 7 2
-------
  6 3 4
```

Use _____ to check your answer.
If 634 – 272 = 362, then 362 + 272 = 634.

Concepts and Skills

Subtract.
Then match those with the same answer.

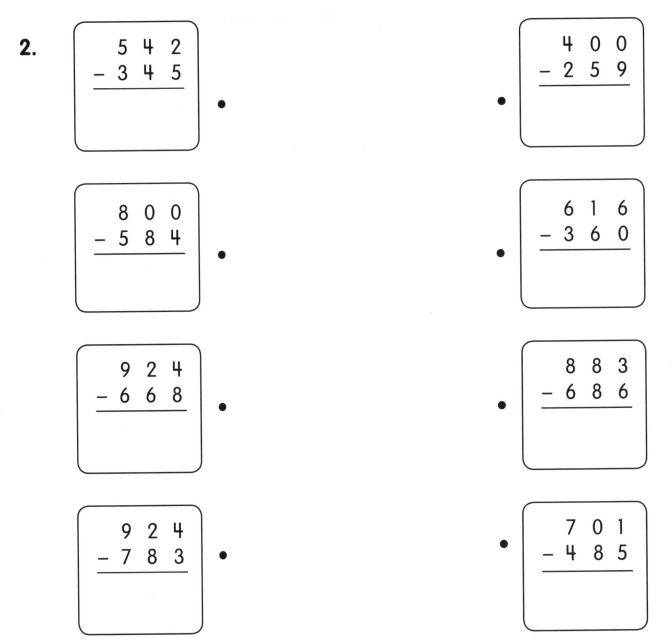

2.

$$\begin{array}{r} 5\ 4\ 2 \\ -\ 3\ 4\ 5 \\ \hline \end{array}$$

$$\begin{array}{r} 4\ 0\ 0 \\ -\ 2\ 5\ 9 \\ \hline \end{array}$$

$$\begin{array}{r} 8\ 0\ 0 \\ -\ 5\ 8\ 4 \\ \hline \end{array}$$

$$\begin{array}{r} 6\ 1\ 6 \\ -\ 3\ 6\ 0 \\ \hline \end{array}$$

$$\begin{array}{r} 9\ 2\ 4 \\ -\ 6\ 6\ 8 \\ \hline \end{array}$$

$$\begin{array}{r} 8\ 8\ 3 \\ -\ 6\ 8\ 6 \\ \hline \end{array}$$

$$\begin{array}{r} 9\ 2\ 4 \\ -\ 7\ 8\ 3 \\ \hline \end{array}$$

$$\begin{array}{r} 7\ 0\ 1 \\ -\ 4\ 8\ 5 \\ \hline \end{array}$$

Problem Solving

Solve.
Show how to check your answer.

3. A supermarket has 412 bottles of apple juice.
123 bottles of apple juice are sold.
How many bottles of apple juice are left?

_____ bottles of apple juice are left.

4. Mr. Smith made 207 sandwiches.
18 sandwiches are tuna.
How many sandwiches are not tuna?

_____ sandwiches are not tuna.

5. The Morgans drive 864 miles in the first week of their vacation.
They drive 178 fewer miles in the second week.
How many miles do they drive in the second week?

They drive _____ miles in the second week.

6. The Health Food Store has 600 jars of strawberry jam.
It has 167 more jars of strawberry jam than blueberry jam.
How many jars of blueberry jam does the store have?

The store has _____ jars of blueberry jam.

CHAPTER 4 Using Bar Models: Addition and Subtraction

Practice 1   Using Part-Part-Whole in Addition and Subtraction

Solve.
Use the bar models to help you.

1. Miss Lucy has 27 students in her morning ballet class.
She has 39 students in her afternoon ballet class.
How many students does she have in both classes?

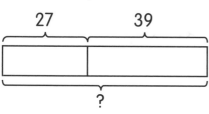

27 + 39 = _____

She has _____ students in both classes.

2. Rani collects 365 beads in January.
She collects 419 beads in April.
How many beads does she collect in January and April?

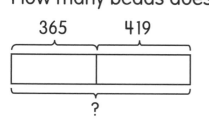   

She collects _____ beads in January and April.

Solve.
Draw bar models to help you.

3. Mr. Jackson drove 427 miles last week.
This week, he drove 215 miles.
How many miles did he drive in the two weeks?

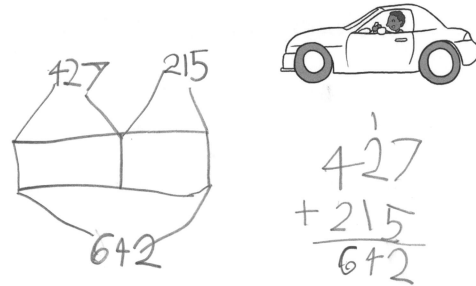

He drove __642__ miles in the two weeks.

4. 143 men and 62 women go to a concert.
How many adults go to the concert?

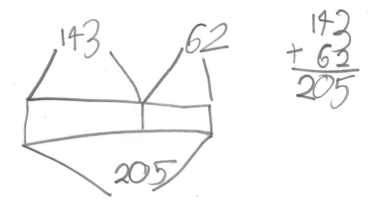

__205__ adults are at the concert.

Name: _____ **Date:** _____

Solve.
Use the bar models to help you.

5. There are 278 people at a camp.
26 of them are teachers and the rest are children.
How many children are there?

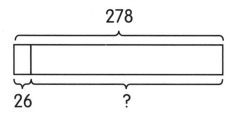

278 − 26 = _____

There are _____ children.

6. Mr. Wilson packs 431 files in two boxes.
He packs 216 files in the first box.
How many files does he pack in the second box?

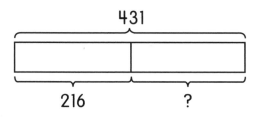

He packs _____ files in the second box.

Solve.
Draw bar models to help you.

7. A letter carrier delivers 999 letters in two days.
The carrier delivers 306 letters on Monday and
the rest of the letters on Tuesday.
How many letters does the carrier deliver on Tuesday?

The carrier delivers _____ letters on Tuesday.

8. A factory makes 674 toys in two days.
325 toys are made on the first day.
How many toys does the factory make on the second day?

The factory makes _____ toys on the second day.

Practice 2   Adding On and Taking Away Sets

Solve.
Use the bar models to help you.

1. Luke has 83 toy cars.
    His brother gives him 52 more toy cars.
    How many toy cars does he have altogether?

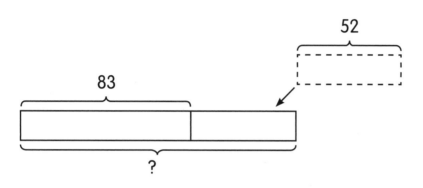

83 + 52 = _____

He has _____ toy cars altogether.

2. Daniel has 228 craft sticks for his project.
    He needs 350 more craft sticks.
    How many craft sticks does he need for his project?

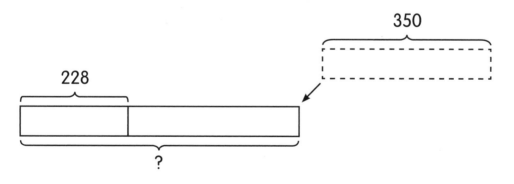

He needs _____ craft sticks for his project.

Solve.
Draw bar models to help you.

3. The Bokil family drives 95 miles on the first day of their trip.
   They drive another 105 miles on the next day.
   How many miles do they drive in the two days?

   They drive _____ miles in the two days.

4. Kayla has 9 puzzles.
   Her mother gives her 8 more puzzles.
   Her uncle buys another 5 puzzles for her.
   How many puzzles does Kayla have now?

   She has _____ puzzles now.

Solve.
Use the bar models to help you.

5. Town Sports has 99 scooters.
The store sells some of them and has 45 scooters left.
How many scooters does Town Sports sell?

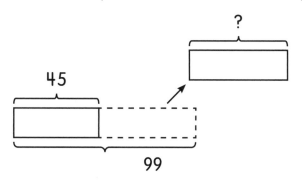

$99 - 45 =$ _____

Town Sports sold _____ scooters.

6. There were 367 bicycles at Ben's bicycle shop.
174 bicycles are rented.
How many bicycles are left?

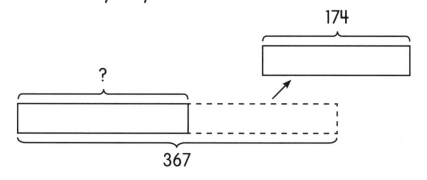

_____ bicycles are left.

Solve.
Draw bar models to help you.

7. Shawn has 405 stickers.
    He gives 278 stickers away.
    How many stickers does he have left?

He has _____ stickers left.

8. There were 282 people in the park on Sunday afternoon.
    In the evening, 199 people went home.
    How many people were left in the park?

_____ people were left in the park.

Practice 3 Comparing Two Sets

Solve.
Complete the bar models to help you.

1. 102 children at a swimming pool do not wear goggles.
23 more children wear goggles than those who do
not wear goggles.
How many children wear goggles?

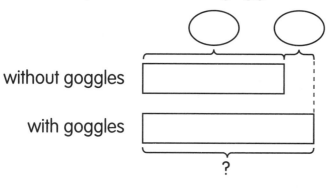

_____ children wear goggles.

2. Alice made 166 ham sandwiches for a party.
She made 77 fewer cheese sandwiches than ham
sandwiches for the party.
How many cheese sandwiches did Alice make?

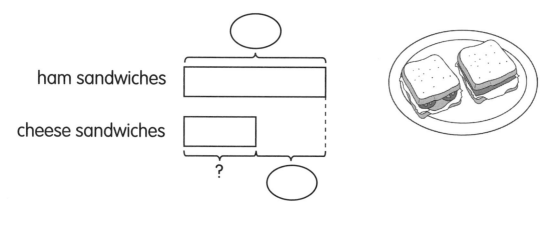

Alice made _____ cheese sandwiches.

Solve.
Draw bar models to help you.

3.   Sam makes 123 party favors.
       Lily makes 87 more party favors than Sam.
       How many party favors does Lily make?

       Lily makes _____ party favors.

4.   952 children watch a funny movie.
       265 fewer adults than children watch the funny movie.
       How many adults watch the funny movie?

_____ adults watch the funny movie.

Name: _____ **Date:** _____

Solve.
Complete the bar models to help you.

5. Mr. Diaz has 347 apple trees in his orchard.
He has 162 more apple trees than peach trees in his orchard.
How many peach trees does Mr. Diaz have in his orchard?

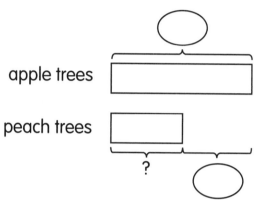

Mr. Diaz has _____ peach trees in his orchard.

6. Shop A sells 97 television sets in December.
It sells 166 fewer television sets than Shop B in December.
How many television sets does Shop B sell in December?

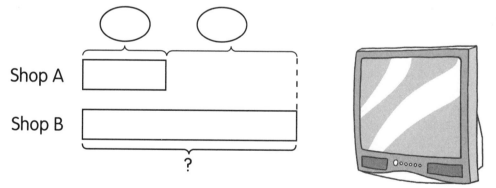

Shop B sells _____ television sets in December.

Solve.
Draw bar models to help you.

7.   The school cook orders 219 hamburgers.
      He orders 120 more hamburgers than hot dogs.
      How many hot dogs does the school cook order?

      The school cook orders _____ hot dogs.

8.   234 flag twirlers march in the Fourth of July parade.
      There are 159 fewer flag twirlers than band members at the parade.
      How many band members are at the parade?

      _____ band members are at the parade.

Practice 4 Real-World Problems: Two-Step Problems

Solve.
Complete the bar models to help you.

1. Mr. Kim has 78 boxes of apples and 130 boxes of oranges.
   He sells some boxes of oranges.
   Now he has 159 boxes of apples and oranges left.

   a. How many boxes of apples and oranges did Mr. Kim have at first?

   b. How many boxes of oranges did Mr. Kim sell?

   a.

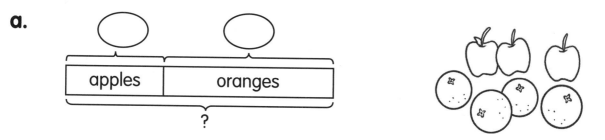

   Mr. Kim had _____ boxes of apples and oranges at first.

   b.

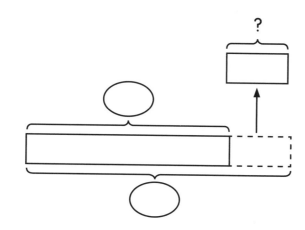

   Mr. Kim sold _____ boxes of oranges.

Solve.
Complete the bar models to help you.

2.   Sophie has 356 stamps in her collection.
      Rita has 192 stamps more than Sophie.
      a.   How many stamps does Rita have?
      b.   How many stamps do they have in all?

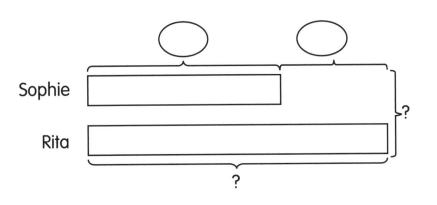

a.   Rita has _____ stamps.

b.   They have _____ stamps in all.

Solve.
Draw bar models to help you.

3.   Kennedy Elementary School has 784 students.
       325 students are boys.

    a.   How many girls are in the school?

    b.   How many more girls than boys are in the school?

    a.   _____ girls are in the school.

    b.   _____ more girls are in the school than boys.

Solve.
Draw bar models to help you.

4.   Club A has 235 male members, and 172 female members.
      45 new members join the club.
      a.   How many members were in the club at first?
      b.   How many members are in the club now?

      a.   _____ members were in the club at first.

      b.   _____ members are in the club now.

5. Kate's grandmother had $245.
She spends $78.
Then she gives $36 to Kate.
How much money does Kate's grandmother have now?

First, find how much she has left after spending $78.

She has _____ now.

Solve.
Draw bar models to help you.

6. There are 147 daisy plants and 32 tulip plants in Nursery X.
    Nursery Y has 66 fewer daisy and tulip plants than Nursery X.
    How many daisy and tulip plants are there in Nursery Y?

There are _____ daisy and tulip plants in Nursery Y.

Math Journal

Write an addition story or a subtraction story for each bar model.
Then solve.

1.

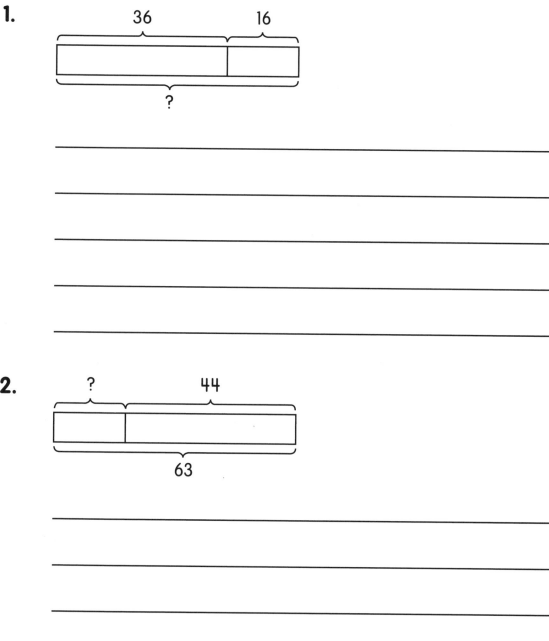

36   16

?

_____

_____

_____

_____

_____

2.

?   44

63

_____

_____

_____

_____

Write an addition story or a subtraction story for the bar model.
Then solve.

3.

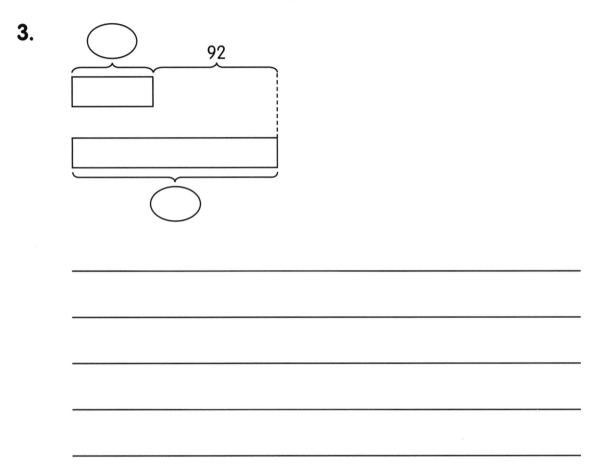

_____

_____

_____

_____

_____

Name: _____ Date: _____

Put On Your Thinking Cap!

Problem Solving

Solve.

1. Sean has 24 fewer toys than Winona.
   After Winona gives some toys to Sean, both of them have
   the same number of toys.
   How many toys does Winona give Sean?

   Winona gives Sean _____ toys.

2. Nadia has 20 more postcards than Pete.
After Nadia gives Pete some postcards,
Pete has 2 more postcards than Nadia.
How many postcards does Nadia give to Pete?

Nadia gives Pete _____ postcards.

Chapter Review/Test

Vocabulary

Fill in the blanks with words from the box.

add	subtract	compare	sets

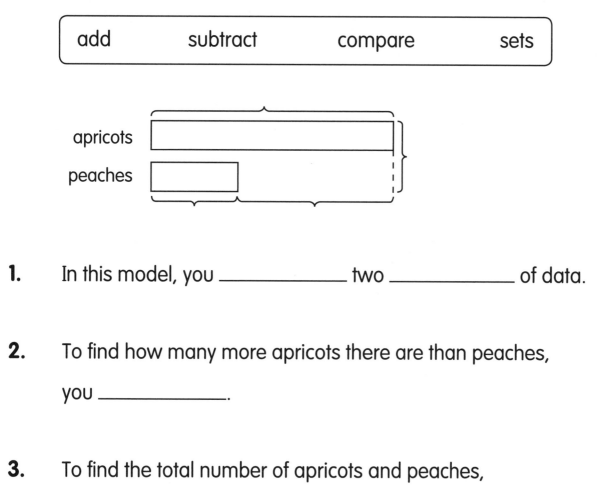

apricots

peaches

1. In this model, you _____ two _____ of data.

2. To find how many more apricots there are than peaches,

    you _____.

3. To find the total number of apricots and peaches,

    you _____.

Concepts and Skills

Fill in each 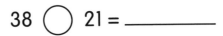 with + or –.

Then fill in the blanks.

4.

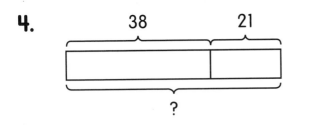

38 ◯ 21 = _____

5.

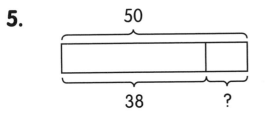

50 ◯ 38 = _____

6.

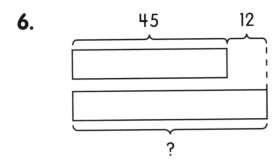

45 ◯ 12 = _____

7.

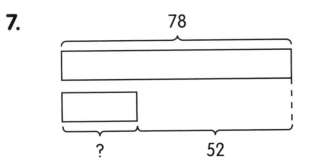

78 ◯ 52 = _____

Problem Solving

Solve.
Draw bar models to help you.

8. A jewelry store has 198 rings and bracelets altogether.
It has 89 bracelets.
How many more rings than bracelets does the store have?

The store has _____ more rings than bracelets.

9. Andy reads 56 more pages of his book on Monday
than on Tuesday.
He reads 125 pages on Monday.
How many pages in all does he read on Monday and Tuesday?

He reads _____ pages in all.

10. An office has 223 workers.
132 of the workers are men.
How many more men work in the office than women?

_____ more men work in the office than women.

11. A furniture shop has 581 tables and chairs in all.
There are 125 tables.
How many more chairs than tables are there in the shop?

There are _____ more chairs than tables in the shop.

Cumulative Review
for Chapters 1 to 4

Concepts and Skills

Write in standard form.

1. Seven hundred sixteen __716__

2. Four hundred five __45 405__

Count on or count back.
Find the missing numbers.

3. 820, 810, 800, _____, _____, _____

4. 600, 700, 800, __900__, __1000__

5. 500, 400, 300, __600__, __700__, __9000__

Find the missing numbers.

6. In 632, the digit __3__ is in the tens place.

7. In 591, the digit 5 is in the __5__ place.

8. 743 = 700 + _____ + 3

9. 200 and 2 make __2002__.

Write > or <.

10. 235 ⟨<⟩ 325   11. 891 ⟨>⟩ 889

Order the numbers from least to greatest.

12.

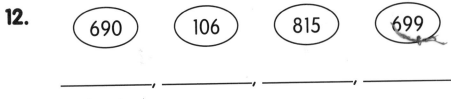

$\underline{\hspace{2cm}}$, $\underline{\hspace{2cm}}$, $\underline{\hspace{2cm}}$, $\underline{\hspace{2cm}}$
least

Find the missing numbers.

13.

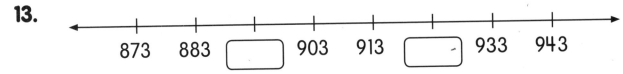

873　　883　　$\boxed{}$　　903　　913　　$\boxed{}$　　933　　943

Fill in the blanks.

14.　1 more than 638 is $\underline{\hspace{2cm}}$.

15.　10 less than 286 is $\underline{\hspace{2cm}}$.

16.　100 more than 899 is $\underline{\hspace{2cm}}$.

17.　$\underline{\hspace{2cm}}$ is 1 less than 360.

18.　$\underline{\hspace{2cm}}$ is 10 more than 890.

19.　$\underline{\hspace{2cm}}$ is 100 less than 1,000.

Complete each pattern.

20.　240, 220, $\underline{\hspace{1.5cm}}$, $\underline{\hspace{1.5cm}}$, 160, $\underline{\hspace{1.5cm}}$, $\underline{\hspace{1.5cm}}$

21.　350, 390, 430, $\underline{\hspace{1.5cm}}$, $\underline{\hspace{1.5cm}}$, $\underline{\hspace{1.5cm}}$, $\underline{\hspace{1.5cm}}$

22.　$\underline{\hspace{1.5cm}}$, $\underline{\hspace{1.5cm}}$, 454, 354, 254, $\underline{\hspace{1.5cm}}$, $\underline{\hspace{1.5cm}}$

Name: _____   **Date:** _____

Add.

23.
```
    2 5 7
  +   4 2
  ───────
    2 9 9
```

24.
```
    2 3 4
  + 7 1 3
  ───────
    9 4 7
```

25.
```
    7 0 8
  +   3 6
  ───────
    7 4 4
```

26.
```
    2 5 6
  + 1 3 8
  ───────
    3 9 4
```

27.
```
    6 5 1
  + 2 8 6
  ───────
    9 3 7
```

28.
```
    6 5 7
  + 1 8 5
  ───────
    8 4 2
```

Subtract.

29.
```
    7 5 9
  -   4 2
  ───────
```

30.
```
    3 6 8
  - 2 1 4
  ───────
```

31.
```
    5 4 1
  - 2 3 8
  ───────
```

32.
```
    4 2 7
  - 1 3 4
  ───────
```

33.
```
    8 3 1
  - 6 9 8
  ───────
```

34.
```
    2 0 0
  -   4 8
  ───────
```

Subtract.
Check by adding.

35.
```
    5 1 0
  - 3 8 5
  ───────
```

36.
```
    4 0 8
  - 2 1 9
  ───────
```

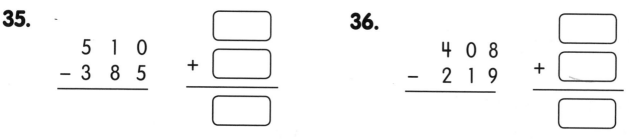

Subtract.
Check by adding.

37. $400 - 57 =$ _____

38. $500 - 493 =$ _____

Find the missing numbers.

39.

```
    2  5  6
 -  ☐  4
 ─────────
    1  6  2
```

40.

```
  ☐  0  8
+ 3  9  9
─────────
  9  0  7
```

Problem Solving

Solve.
Draw bar models to help you.
Check your answers.

41. Manuel drives 215 miles on Monday.
He drives 685 miles on Tuesday.
How many miles does he drive in all?

He drives _____ miles in all.

42. Mrs. King has $200 in the bank.
She spends $45.
How much does she have left?

She has $_____ left.

© Marshall Cavendish International (Singapore) Private Limited.

Solve.
Draw bar models to help you.
Check your answers.

43.   Jeremy has 430 black beads.
He has 50 more red beads than black beads.
How many red beads does he have?

He has _____ red beads.

44.   There are 356 sheep on a farm.
There are 100 fewer cows than sheep.
How many cows are there?

There are _____ cows.

45.   Mike has 515 stickers in his album.
Shateel has 488 stickers in his.
Who has more stickers?
How many more stickers?

_____ has more stickers.

_____ more stickers.

Solve.
Draw bar models to help you.
Check your answers.

46. Nick scores 715 points in a game.
He scores 100 fewer points than his sister.
How many points does his sister score?

His sister scores _____ points.

47. Beth reads for 60 minutes in the morning.
She reads for 42 minutes at night.
How many minutes does she read in all?

Beth reads for _____ minutes in all.

Solve.
Draw bar models to help you.
Check your answers.

48. 339 passengers are on a train.
196 of them are children.
The others are adults.
How many adults are on the train?

There are _____ adults on the train.

49. The Hat Store sold 265 caps last week.
It sold 97 fewer caps this week.
  a. How many caps did the Hat Store sell this week?
  b. How many caps did the Hat Store sell for the two weeks?

  a. The Hat Store sold _____ caps this week.

  b. The Hat Store sold _____ caps for the two weeks.

Solve.
Draw bar models to help you.
Check your answers.

50. The theater sold 343 tickets on Friday.
This is 192 fewer tickets than those sold on Saturday.
How many tickets were sold altogether?

_____ tickets were sold altogether.

51. 365 people watch a show on Monday.
78 more people watch the show on Tuesday.
105 more people watch the show on Tuesday than on Wednesday.
How many people watch the show on Wednesday?

_____ people watch the show on Wednesday.

Name: _____ Date: _____

Multiplication and Division

Practice 1   How to Multiply

Count, add, and write the number of animals in each group.
Then multiply.

— **Example** —

$3 + 3 + 3 + 3 + 3 + 3 =$ _____ *18*

6 threes = _____ *18* $6 \times 3 =$ _____ *18*

1.

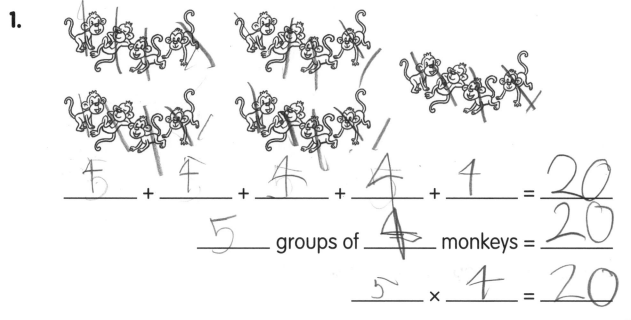

_____ + _____ + _____ + _____ + _____ = _____
  4   *4*   *4*   *4*   *4*   *20*
                                                20

_____ groups of _____ monkeys = _____
  5   *4*   *20*

_____ × _____ = _____
  5   *4*   *20*

Count, add, and write the number of animals in each group. Then multiply.

2.

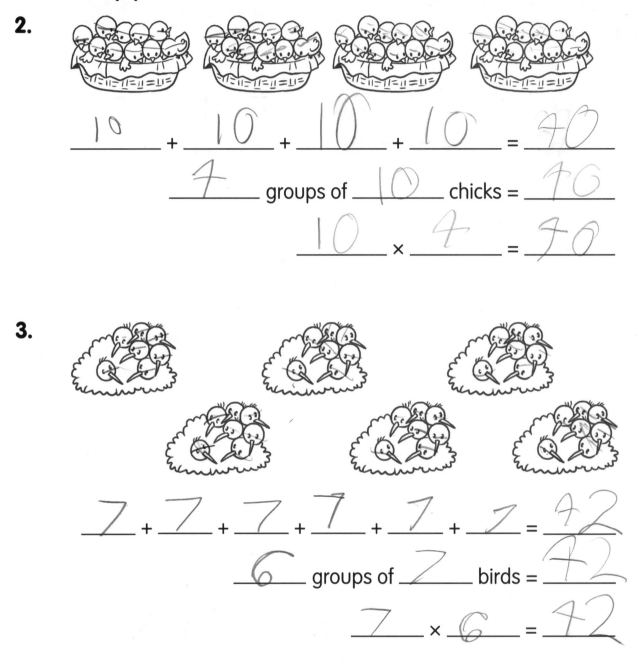

_____10_____ + _____10_____ + _____10_____ + _____10_____ = _____40_____

_____4_____ groups of _____10_____ chicks = _____40_____

_____10_____ × _____4_____ = _____40_____

3.

_____7_____ + _____7_____ + _____7_____ + _____7_____ + _____7_____ + _____7_____ = _____42_____

_____6_____ groups of _____7_____ birds = _____42_____

_____7_____ × _____6_____ = _____42_____

Practice 2 How to Multiply

Look at the addition and multiplication sentences.
Fill in the blanks.

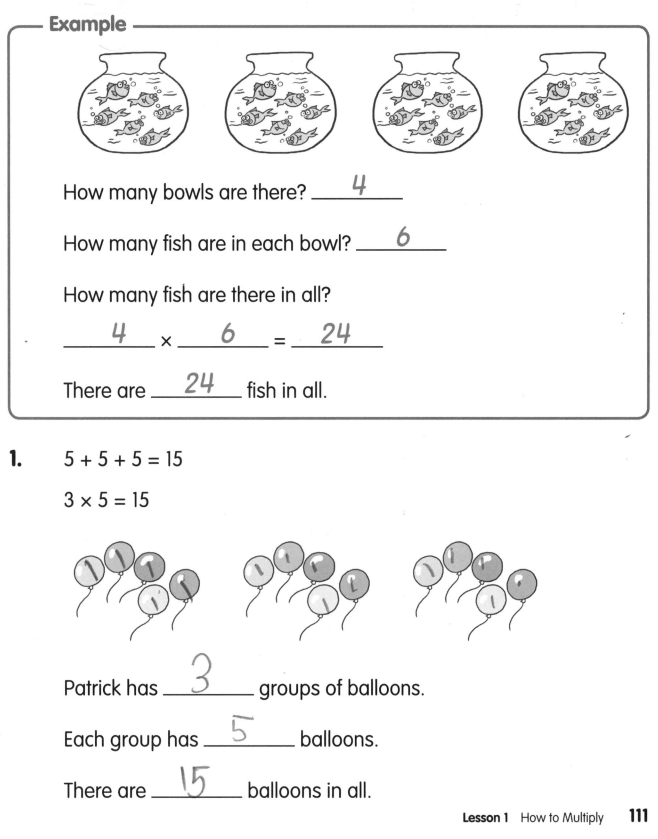

Example

How many bowls are there? ____4____

How many fish are in each bowl? ____6____

How many fish are there in all?

____4____ × ____6____ = ____24____

There are ____24____ fish in all.

1. 5 + 5 + 5 = 15

3 × 5 = 15

Patrick has ____3____ groups of balloons.

Each group has ____5____ balloons.

There are ____15____ balloons in all.

Write the addition and multiplication sentences.
Fill in the blanks.

2.

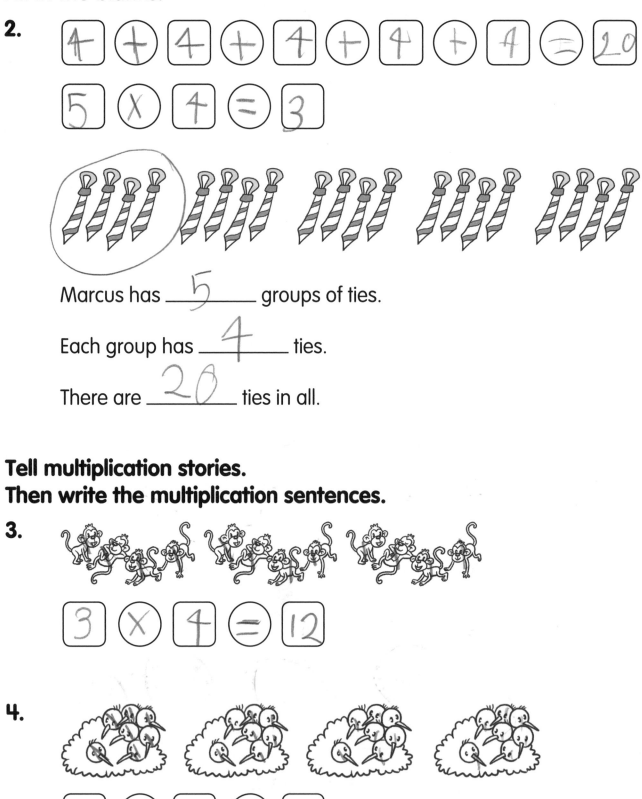

4 + 4 + 4 + 4 + 4 = 20

5 X 4 = 3

Marcus has ___5___ groups of ties.

Each group has ___4___ ties.

There are ___20___ ties in all.

Tell multiplication stories.
Then write the multiplication sentences.

3.

3 X 4 = 12

4.

4 X 7 = 28

Practice 3   How to Divide

Find the number of items in each group.

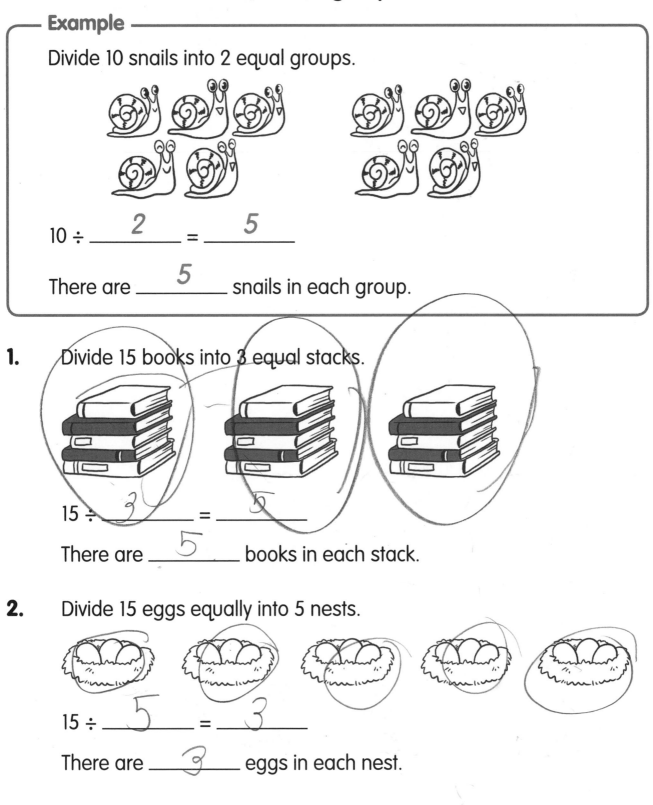

Example

Divide 10 snails into 2 equal groups.

10 ÷ _____2_____ = _____5_____

There are _____5_____ snails in each group.

1.   Divide 15 books into 3 equal stacks.

15 ÷ _____3_____ = _____5_____

There are _____5_____ books in each stack.

2.   Divide 15 eggs equally into 5 nests.

15 ÷ _____5_____ = _____3_____

There are _____3_____ eggs in each nest.

Find the number of groups.
Fill in the blanks.

Example

Divide 15 pancakes so there are 3 pancakes in each group.

Subtract groups of 3 until there is nothing left.

15 – ___3___ – ___3___ – ___3___ – ___3___ – ___3___ = ___0___

How many times do you subtract groups of 3? ___5___

15 ÷ 3 = ___5___

There are ___5___ groups.

3. Divide 12 beads into groups of 4.

Subtract groups of 4 until there are none left.

12 – ___4___ – ___4___ – ___4___ = 0

How many times did you subtract groups of 4? ___3___

12 ÷ ___4___ = ___3___

There are ___3___ groups of 4 beads.

4. Divide 14 frozen yogurt cones into groups of 7.

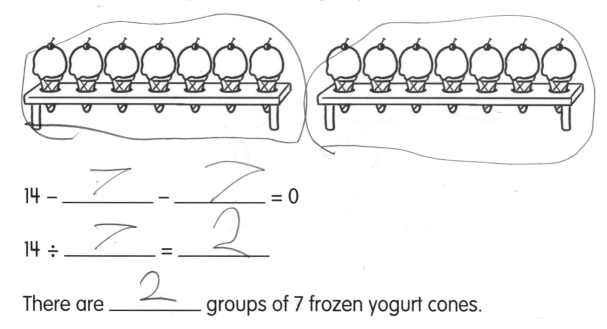

14 – _____7_____ – _____7_____ = 0

14 ÷ _____7_____ = ___2___

There are ___2___ groups of 7 frozen yogurt cones.

5. Put 20 oranges onto plates with 5 on each plate.

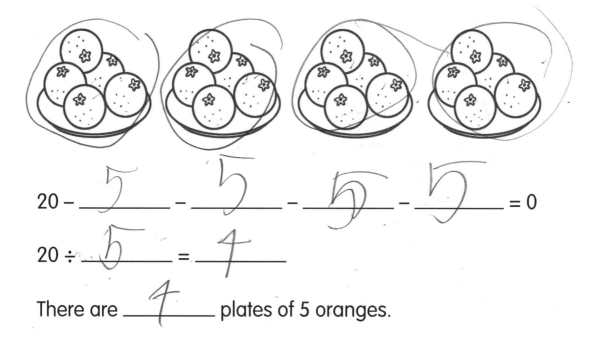

20 – ___5___ – ___5___ – ___5___ – ___5___ = 0

20 ÷ ___5___ = ___4___

There are ___4___ plates of 5 oranges.

6. Put 24 glasses onto trays with 6 on each tray.

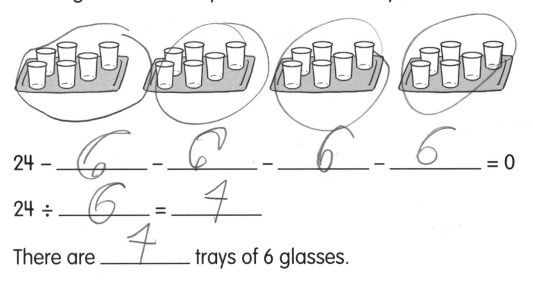

24 – __6__ – __6__ – __6__ – __6__ = 0

24 ÷ __6__ = __4__

There are __4__ trays of 6 glasses.

7. Put 8 cookies onto plates with 2 on each tray.

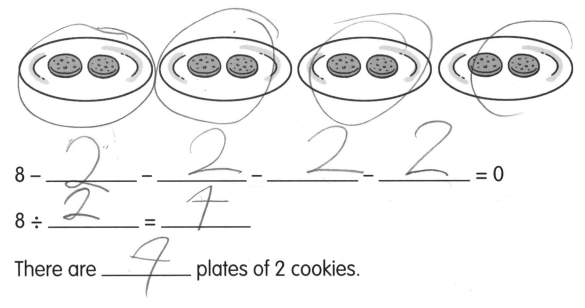

8 – __2__ – __2__ – __2__ – __2__ = 0

8 ÷ __2__ = __4__

There are __4__ plates of 2 cookies.

Practice 4   Real-World Problems: Multiplication and Division

Solve.

1.   There are 2 plates.
Each plate has 5 strawberries.
How many strawberries are there?

5 + 5 = ___10___

2 × 5 = ___10___

There are ___10___ strawberries.

2.   There are 6 bags.
Each bag has 3 pockets.
How many pockets are there?

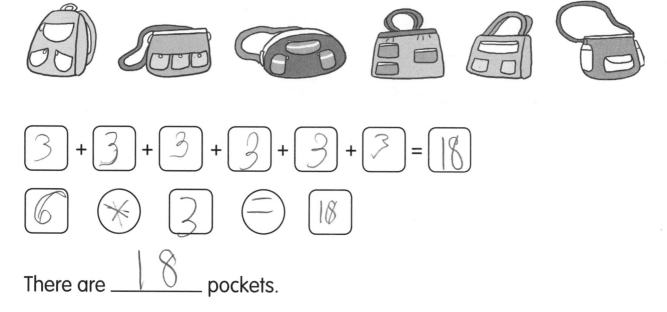

[3] + [3] + [3] + [3] + [3] + [3] = [18]

[6] (*) [3] (−) [18]

There are ___18___ pockets.

3. Tim has 4 jars.
There are 6 marbles in each jar.
How many marbles does Tim have altogether?

$$\boxed{6} + \boxed{6} + \boxed{6} + \boxed{6} = \boxed{24}$$

$$\boxed{4} \times \boxed{6} = \boxed{24}$$

Tim has ___24___ marbles altogether.

4. Yanthi has 5 boxes.
There are 8 pencils in each box.
How many pencils does she have altogether?

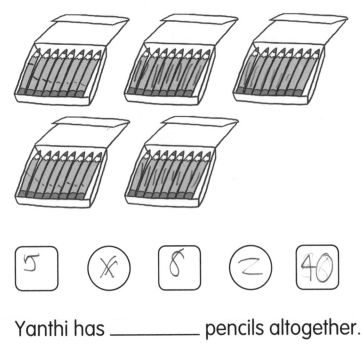

$$\boxed{5} \ \boxed{\times} \ \boxed{8} \ \boxed{=} \ \boxed{40}$$

Yanthi has _____ pencils altogether.

5.

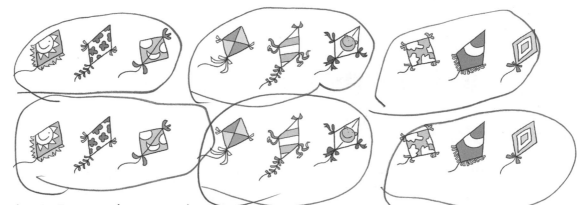

Aunt Emma buys 18 kites.

She gives 3 kites to each of her nephews.

How many nephews does Aunt Emma have?

$$\underline{18} - \underline{3} - \underline{3} - \underline{3} - \underline{3} - \underline{3} - \underline{3} = 0$$

$$\underline{18} \div \underline{3} = \underline{6}$$

Aunt Emma has ____6____ nephews.

6.

Mr. O'Brien catches 28 fish.

He puts 7 fish in each bucket.

How many buckets does he have?

$$\underline{28} - \underline{7} - \underline{7} - \underline{7} - \underline{7} = 0$$

$$\underline{28} \div \underline{7} = \underline{4}$$

He has ____4____ buckets.

Math Journal

Look at the picture.

Put 12 stars into equal groups in different ways.
What are the multiplication sentences and division sentences that you can write?
Draw circles around the stars to help you.

☆ ☆ ☆ ☆ ☆ ☆ ☆ ☆ ☆ ☆ ☆ ☆

Put On Your Thinking Cap!

Challenging Practice

Maya is making silly stuffed animals.
Study the number of eyes each stuffed animal has.
Find a pattern.
Then draw the eyes Maya will put on the last two stuffed animals.

Put On Your Thinking Cap!

Problem Solving

An open jar has 36 sugar cubes inside.
Mighty Ant takes 4 days to carry all the sugar cubes back to his nest.
He carries the same number of sugar cubes each day.
How many sugar cubes does he carry each day?

I can solve this problem by drawing a picture or by acting it out with cubes.

Chapter Review/Test
Vocabulary
Match.

1.

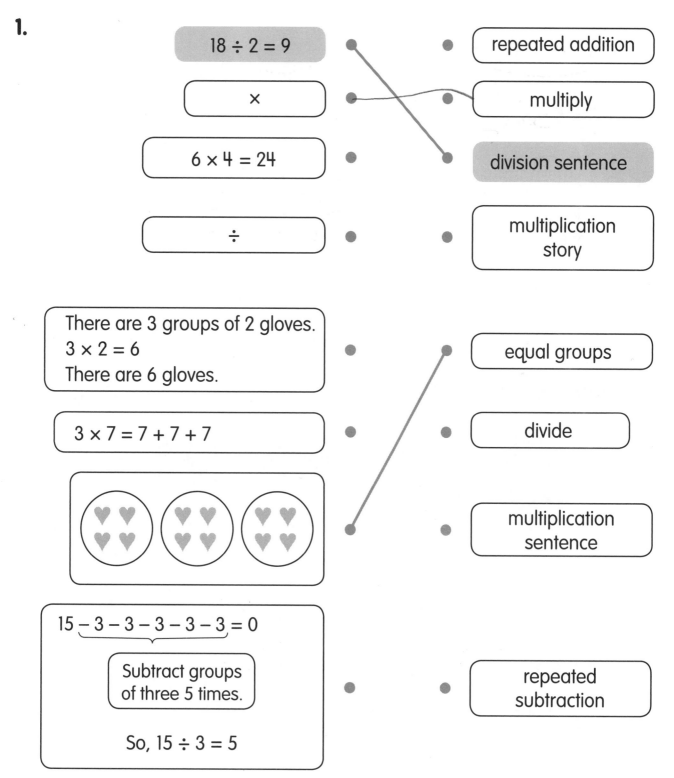

$18 \div 2 = 9$

$\times$

$6 \times 4 = 24$

$\div$

repeated addition

multiply

division sentence

multiplication story

There are 3 groups of 2 gloves.
$3 \times 2 = 6$
There are 6 gloves.

$3 \times 7 = 7 + 7 + 7$

equal groups

divide

multiplication sentence

$15 - 3 - 3 - 3 - 3 - 3 = 0$

Subtract groups of three 5 times.

So, $15 \div 3 = 5$

repeated subtraction

Concepts and Skills

Fill in the ◯ **with +, −, ×, or ÷.**

2. 6 groups of 2 = 6 ⊗ 2

3. 8 ⊗ 4 = 32

4. 3 × 5 = 5 ⊕ 5 ⊕ 5

5. 20 ⊖ 4 ⊖ 4 ⊖ 4 ⊖ 4 ⊖ 4 = 0

6. 20 ⊘ 5 = 4

7. 15 ⊘ 3 = 5

Find the missing numbers.

8.

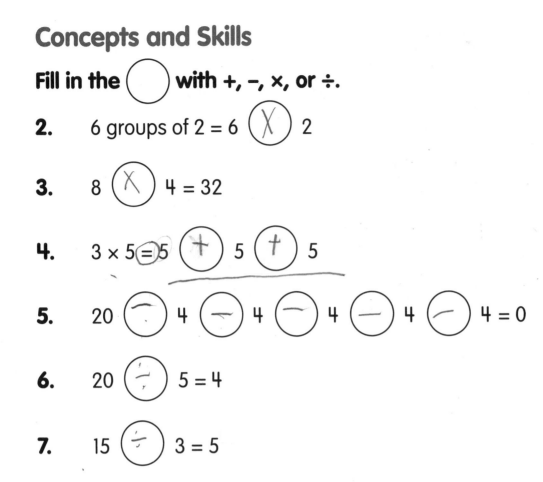

_____4_____ groups of _____3_____ = _____12_____

4 × 3 = __12__.

There are __12__ bees on the flowers in all.

9.

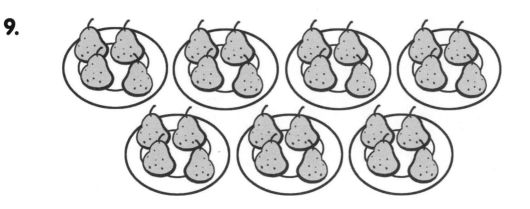

$7 \times 4 =$ ___28___

There are ___28___ pears on the plates in all.

10.

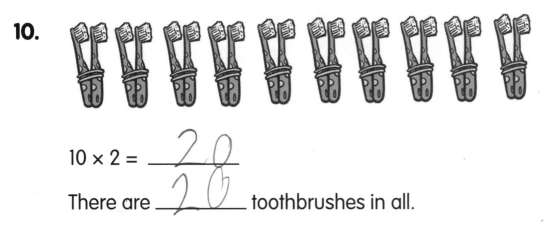

$10 \times 2 =$ ___28___

There are ___28___ toothbrushes in all.

11.

___5___ × ___7___ = ___35___

There are ___35___ buttons in all.

Find the missing numbers.

12. Divide 8 bananas onto 4 plates equally.

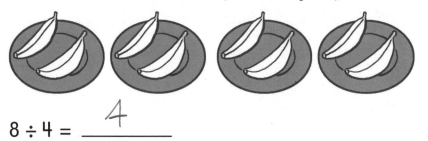

$8 \div 4 =$ _____4_____

13. Divide 20 marbles into 5 equal groups.

$20 \div 5 =$ _____4_____

14. Divide 18 stamps into groups of 2.

$18 \div 2 =$ _____9_____

15. Divide 24 almonds into groups of 3.

$24 \div 3 =$ _____8_____

Name: _____ **Date:** _____

Problem Solving
Solve.

16. Every day, Mr. Smith collects 3 eggs from his chickens.
How many eggs does he collect in a week?

3N = 21

Mr. Smith collects __21__ eggs in a week.

17. There are 3 baskets.
Each basket contains 4 loaves of bread.
How many loaves of bread are there in all?

3 X 4 = 12

There are __12__ loaves of bread in all.

18. Meg has 35 stickers.
She has an album with 5 pages.
She puts an equal number of stickers on each page.
How many stickers are on each page?

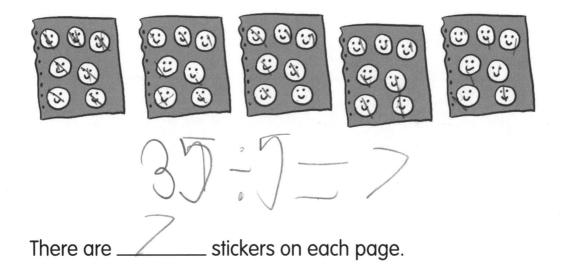

$35 \div 5 = 7$

There are ____7____ stickers on each page.

19. Mrs. Barker has 30 star stickers.
She gives each student 5 star stickers.
How many students are there?

There are ____6____ students.

CHAPTER 6 Multiplication Tables of 2, 5, and 10

Practice 1   Multiplying 2: Skip-Counting

Color the shapes.
Use the same color for the shapes that have the same value.

1.

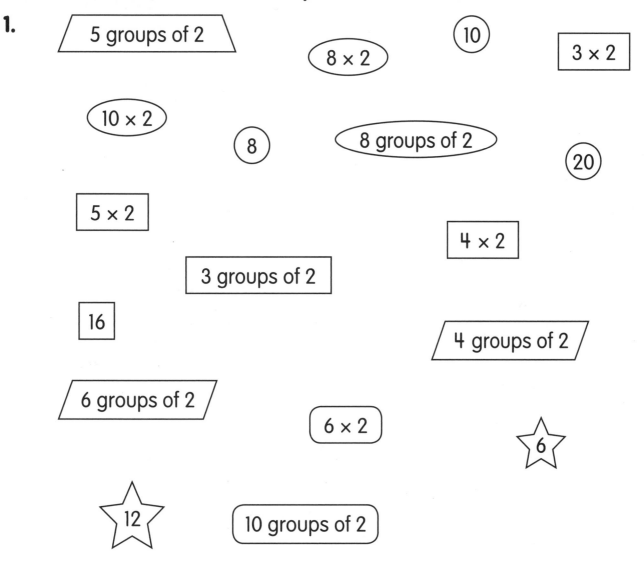

Count by 2s.
Then fill in the blanks.

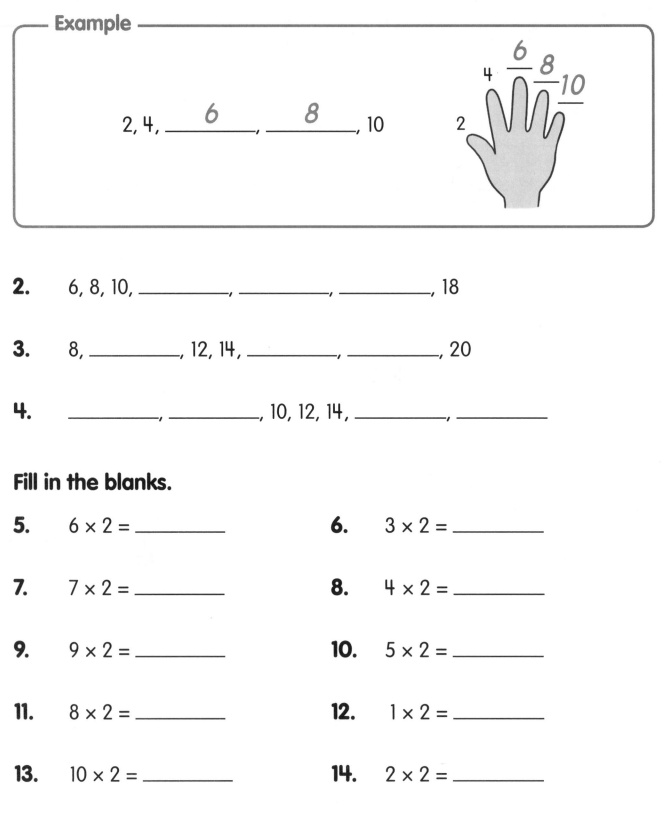

Example

2, 4, _____6_____, _____8_____, 10

4 ⟶ 6 8 10

2

2. 6, 8, 10, _____, _____, _____, 18

3. 8, _____, 12, 14, _____, _____, 20

4. _____, _____, 10, 12, 14, _____, _____

Fill in the blanks.

5. 6 × 2 = _____

6. 3 × 2 = _____

7. 7 × 2 = _____

8. 4 × 2 = _____

9. 9 × 2 = _____

10. 5 × 2 = _____

11. 8 × 2 = _____

12. 1 × 2 = _____

13. 10 × 2 = _____

14. 2 × 2 = _____

Practice 2   Multiplying 2: Using Dot Paper

Use dot paper to solve.

1. There are 4 bags.
2 rolls are in each bag.
How many rolls are there in all?

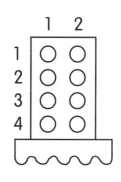

$4 \times 2 =$ _____

There are _____ rolls in all.

2. 6 bicycles are in the shop.
Each bicycle has 2 wheels.
How many wheels are there in all?

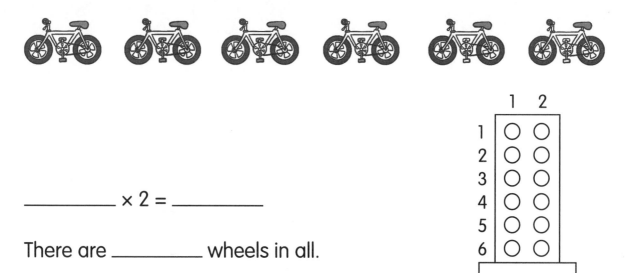

_____ $\times 2 =$ _____

There are _____ wheels in all.

Use dot paper to solve.

3. Mrs. Smith buys 5 burgers for her children.
Each burger costs $2.
How much do the 5 burgers cost in all?

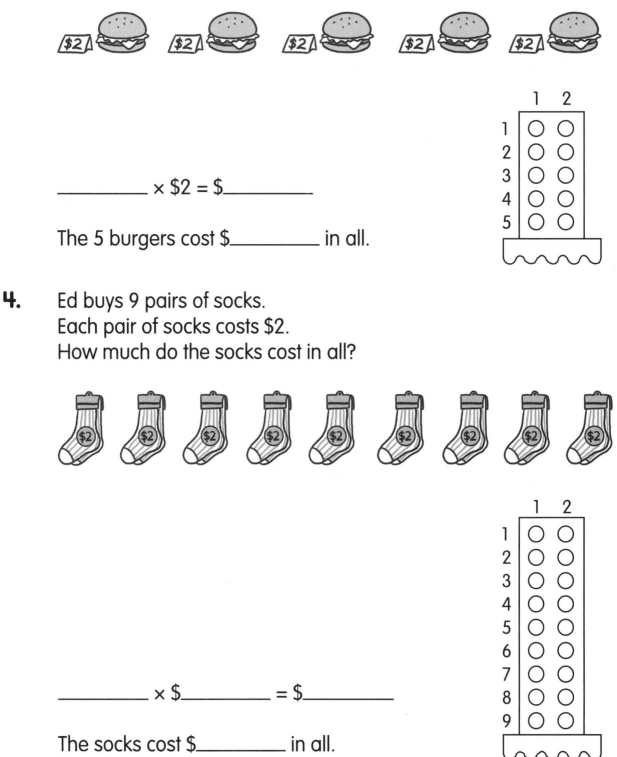

_____ × $2 = $_____

The 5 burgers cost $_____ in all.

4. Ed buys 9 pairs of socks.
Each pair of socks costs $2.
How much do the socks cost in all?

_____ × $_____ = $_____

The socks cost $_____ in all.

Name: _____ Date: _____

Use dot paper to fill in the blanks.

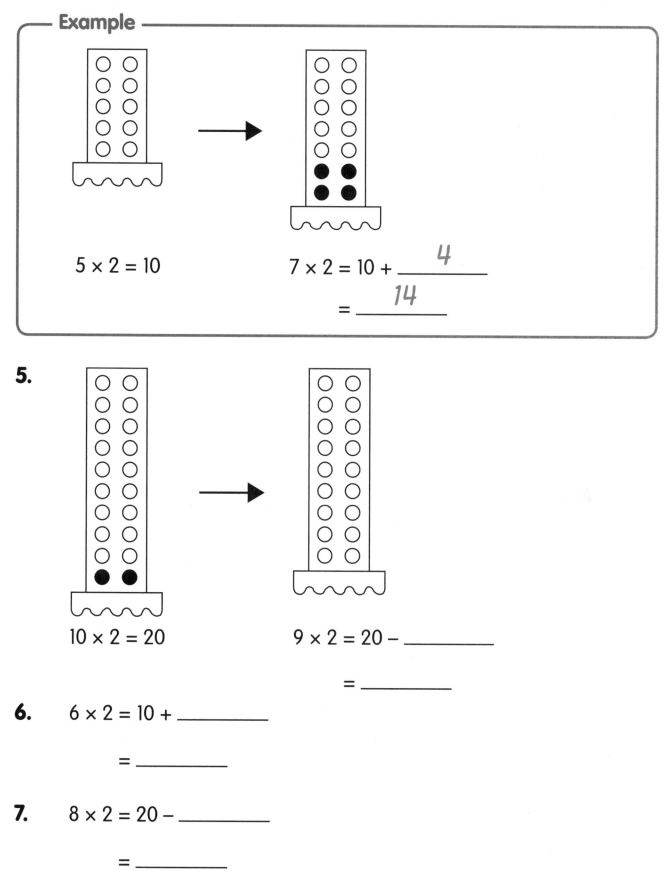

Example

$5 \times 2 = 10$

$7 \times 2 = 10 + \underline{\quad 4 \quad}$

$= \underline{\quad 14 \quad}$

5.

$10 \times 2 = 20$

$9 \times 2 = 20 - \underline{\qquad}$

$= \underline{\qquad}$

6. $6 \times 2 = 10 + \underline{\qquad}$

$= \underline{\qquad}$

7. $8 \times 2 = 20 - \underline{\qquad}$

$= \underline{\qquad}$

Use dot paper to find the missing numbers.

Example

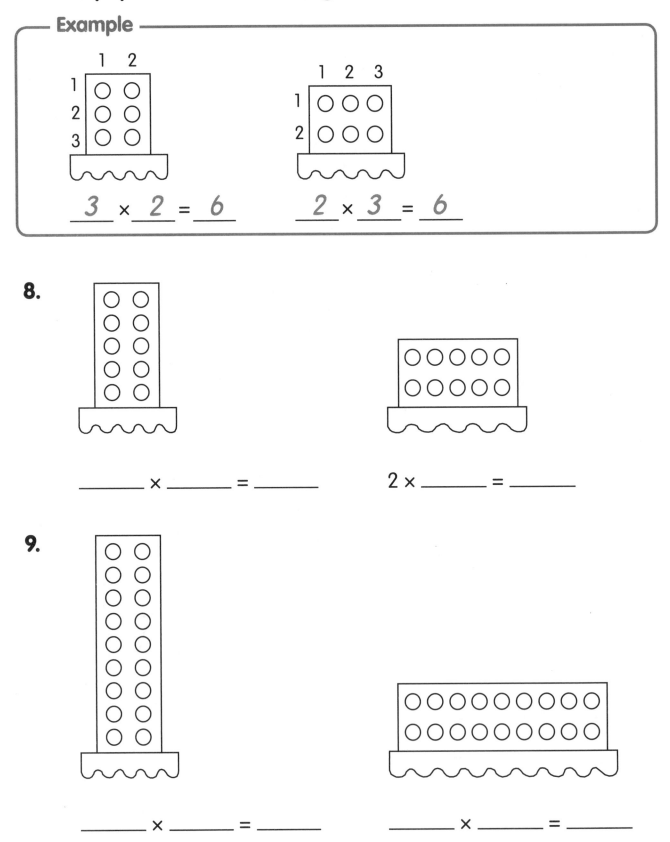

$$\underline{3} \times \underline{2} = \underline{6}$$

$$\underline{2} \times \underline{3} = \underline{6}$$

8.

_____ × _____ = _____

2 × _____ = _____

9.

_____ × _____ = _____

_____ × _____ = _____

Name: _____ Date: _____

Practice 3 Multiplying 5: Skip-Counting

Jon is skip-counting by 5s.
He shades each number he counts on a hundreds chart.
He misses some numbers.
Circle the numbers he misses.

1.

1	2	3	4	5	6	7	8	9	10
11	12	13	14	15	16	17	18	19	20
21	22	23	24	25	26	27	28	29	30
31	32	33	34	35	36	37	38	39	40
41	42	43	44	45	46	47	48	49	50
51	52	53	54	55	56	57	58	59	60
61	62	63	64	65	66	67	68	69	70
71	72	73	74	75	76	77	78	79	80
81	82	83	84	85	86	87	88	89	90
91	92	93	94	95	96	97	98	99	100

Find the missing numbers.

Example

3 groups of 5 = ____3____ × 5

= ____15____

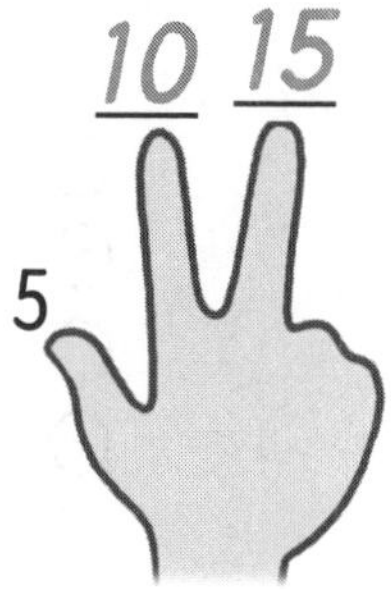

10 15

5

2.   4 groups of 5 = _____ × 5

= _____

___ ___

___

5

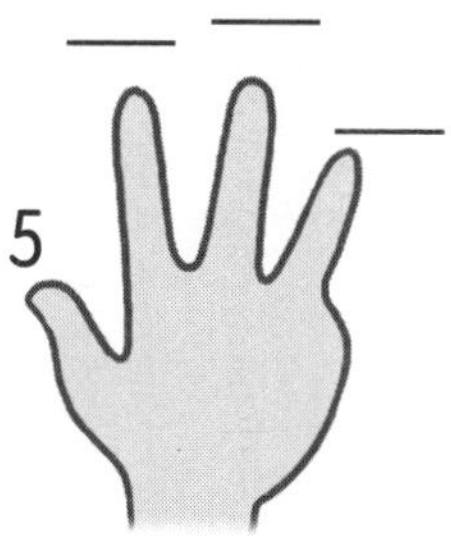

3. 5 groups of 5 = _____ × _____

= _____

4. 7 groups of 5 = _____ × _____

= _____

5. 8 groups of 5 = _____ × _____

= _____

6. 9 groups of 5 = _____ × _____

= _____

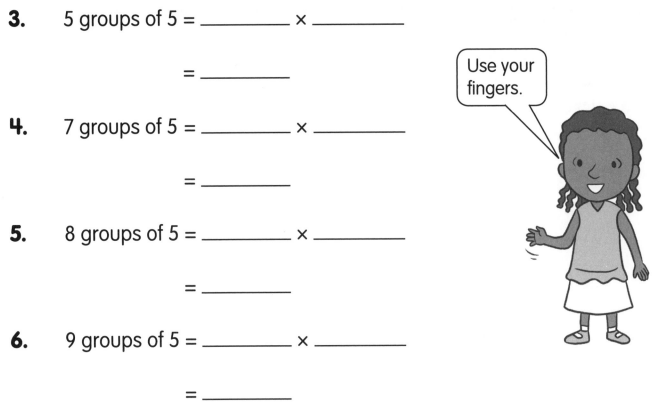

Use your fingers.

Count by 5s.
Then fill in the blanks.

7. 5, 10, 15, 20, 25, _____

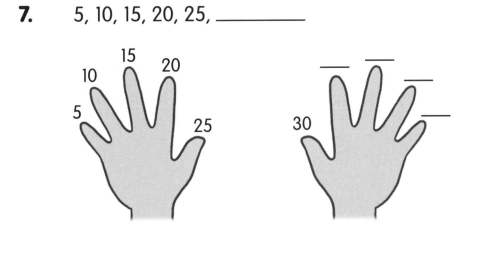

8. 20, 25, _____, _____, _____, _____, _____

Name: _____ **Date:** _____

Count by 5s.
Then fill in the blanks.

9. 20, _____, 30, _____, 40, 45

10. _____, _____, 25, 30, 35, _____, _____, _____

Fill in the blanks.

11. $3 \times 5 =$ _____

12. $2 \times 5 =$ _____

13. $6 \times 5 =$ _____

14. $8 \times 5 =$ _____

15. $9 \times 5 =$ _____

16. $7 \times 5 =$ _____

17. $5 \times 5 =$ _____

18. $10 \times 5 =$ _____

Solve.

19. Three children raise both hands.
There are 5 fingers on each hand.
How many fingers do they raise in all?

$6 \times 5 =$ _____

They raise _____ fingers in all.

20. Jeff buys 7 books at the bookstore.
Each book costs $5.
How much does Jeff pay for the 7 books?

_____ × $_____ = $_____

He pays $_____ for the 7 books.

21. There are 9 trays on the counter.
There are 5 plates on each tray.
How many plates are there in all?

_____ × _____ = _____

There are _____ plates in all.

Practice 4   Multiplying 5: Using Dot Paper

Use dot paper to solve.

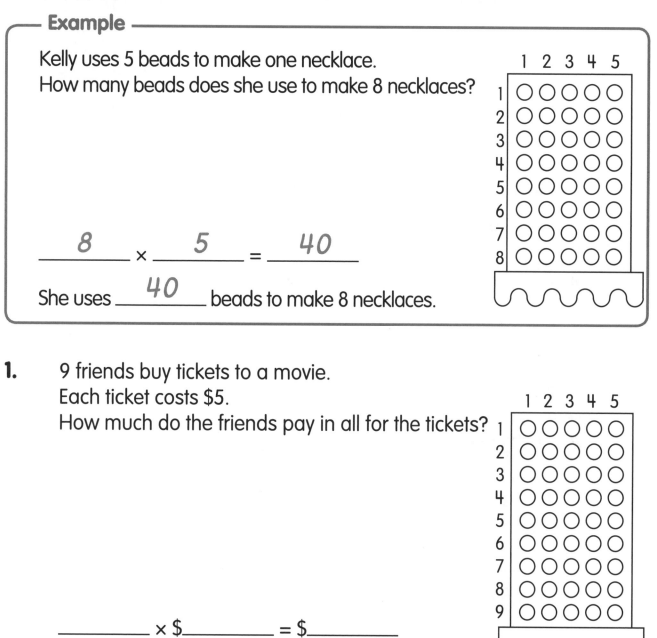

Example

Kelly uses 5 beads to make one necklace.
How many beads does she use to make 8 necklaces?

_____8_____ × _____5_____ = _____40_____

She uses _____40_____ beads to make 8 necklaces.

1.   9 friends buy tickets to a movie.
Each ticket costs $5.
How much do the friends pay in all for the tickets?

_____ × $_____ = $_____

They pay $_____ in all for the tickets.

2. Ellen packs some books into 10 boxes.
She packs 5 books into each box.
How many books does she pack in all?

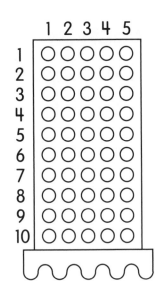

_____ × _____ = _____

She packs _____ books into 10 boxes.

Multiply.
Color the dots to help you.

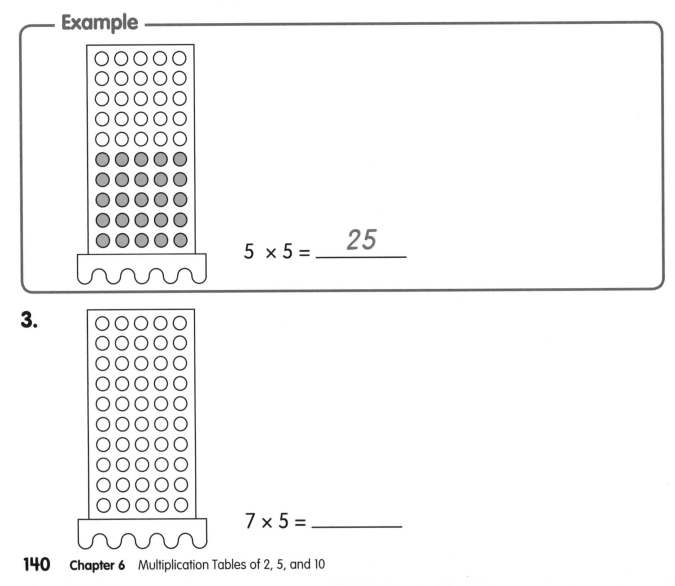

Example

$5 \times 5 =$ ____25____

3.

$7 \times 5 =$ _____

Multiply.
Color the dots to help you.

4.

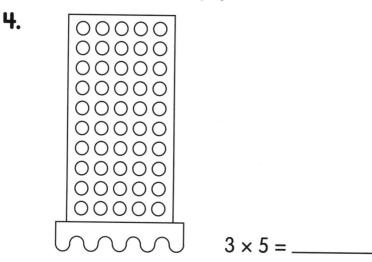

$3 \times 5 =$ _____

Use dot paper to fill in the blanks.

5.

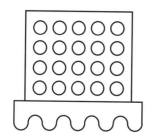

_____ × _____ = _____

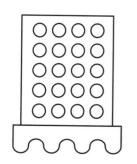

_____ × _____ = _____

Use dot paper to fill in the blanks.

6.

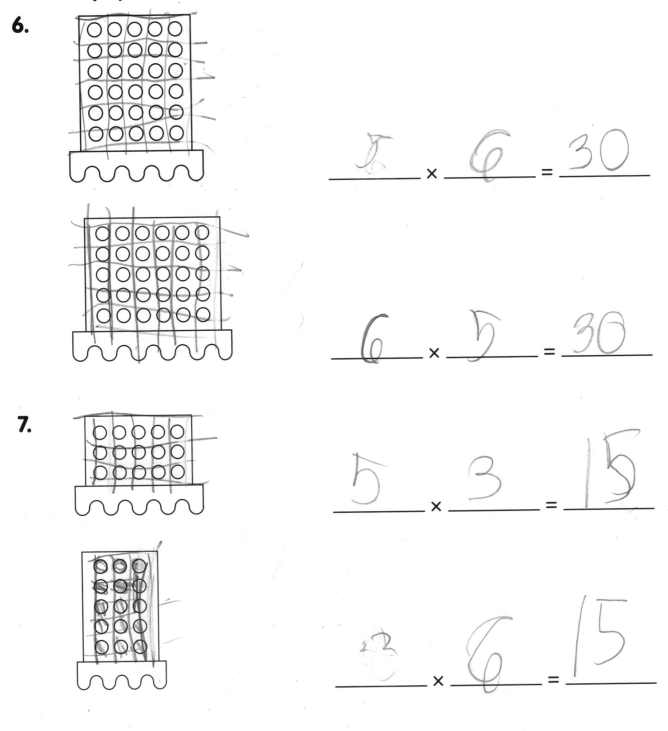

$\underline{5} \times \underline{6} = \underline{30}$

$\underline{6} \times \underline{5} = \underline{30}$

7.

$\underline{5} \times \underline{3} = \underline{15}$

$\underline{3} \times \underline{6} = \underline{15}$

Practice 5 Multiplying 10: Skip-Counting and Using Dot Paper

The numbers below the chart follow a pattern.
Use the hundreds chart to find the missing numbers.

1.

1	2	3	4	5	6	7	8	9	10
11	12	13	14	15	16	17	18	19	20
21	22	23	24	25	26	27	28	29	30
31	32	33	34	35	36	37	38	39	40
41	42	43	44	45	46	47	48	49	50
51	52	53	54	55	56	57	58	59	60
61	62	63	64	65	66	67	68	69	70
71	72	73	74	75	76	77	78	79	80
81	82	83	84	85	86	87	88	89	90
91	92	93	94	95	96	97	98	99	100

10, _20_, _30_, 40, 50, _60_,

70, _80_, 90, _100_

Use patterns to fill in the blanks.

Example

$1 \times 1 =$ _1_

$1 \times 10 =$ _10_

2. $2 \times 1 =$ _2_

$2 \times 10 =$ _20_

3. $3 \times 1 =$ _3_

$3 \times 10 =$ _30_

Use patterns to fill in the blanks.

4. 4×1 = _____   5. 5×1 = _____

     4×10 = _____ 5×10 = _____

6. 6×10 = _____   7. 7×10 = _____

Solve.

8.   There are 4 bundles of sticks.
     Each bundle has 10 sticks.
     How many sticks are there in all?

     4×10 = _____

     There are _____ sticks in all.

9.   Megan makes 6 bracelets.
     She needs 10 beads to make one bracelet.
     How many beads are needed to make the 6 bracelets?

     _____ $\times 10$ = _____

     _____ beads are needed to make the 6 bracelets.

Solve.

10. During sports day, 10 children form a group for a relay race.
How many children are there in 8 groups?

_____ × 10 = _____

There are _____ children in 8 groups.

11. The school band has 10 violins.
Each violin has 4 strings on it.
How many strings are on the 10 violins?

_____ × _____ = _____

There are _____ strings on the 10 violins.

Use dot paper to multiply.

12.

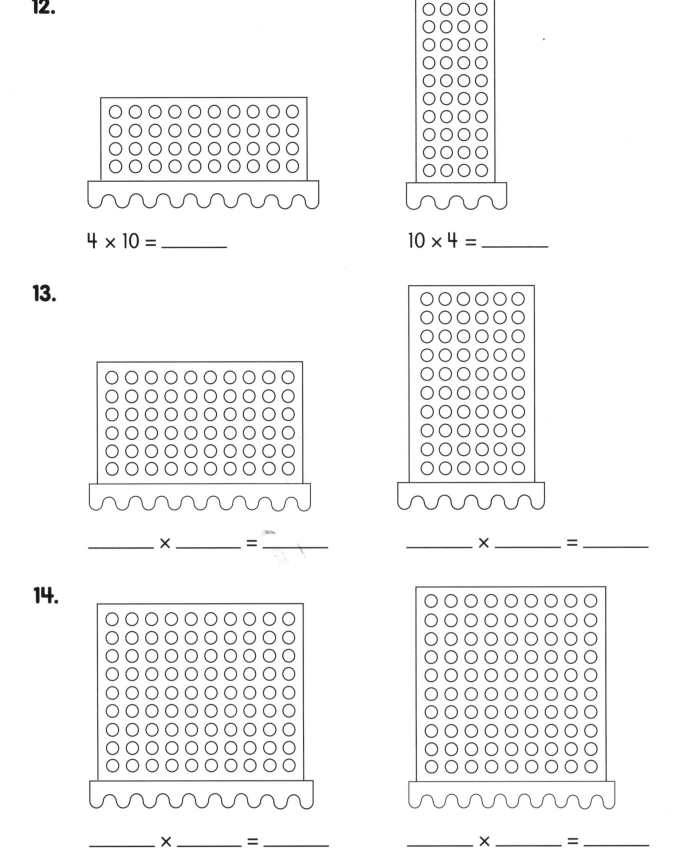

$4 \times 10 =$ _____

$10 \times 4 =$ _____

13.

_____ $\times$ _____ $=$ _____

_____ $\times$ _____ $=$ _____

14.

_____ $\times$ _____ $=$ _____

_____ $\times$ _____ $=$ _____

Practice 6 Odd and Even Numbers

Circle groups of 2.
Write the number.
Then fill in the blank with *odd* or *even*.

— Example —

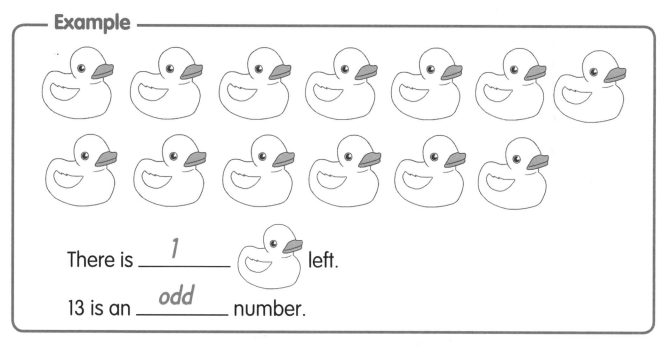

There is _____1_____ left.

13 is an _____odd_____ number.

1. Is 20 an odd or even number?
Circle groups of 2.
Then write *odd* or *even*.

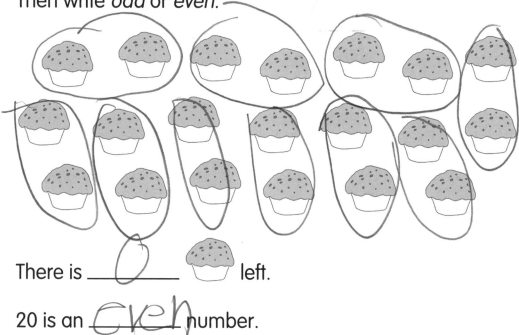

There is _____ left.

20 is an __even__ number.

2. Draw 26 hearts.
Then circle groups of 2.
Is 26 an odd or even number?

26 is an _____ number.

3. Draw 19 flowers.
Then circle groups of 2.

19 is an _____ number.

Complete.
Use numbers that are the same.

4. $8 = 4 +$ _____

5. $12 =$ _____ $+ 6$

6. $10 =$ _____ $+$ _____

7. $22 =$ _____ $+$ _____

Math Journal

$5 diary

$2 pen

$10 dictionary

Look at the pictures.
Write multiplication stories.
Use multiplication tables of 5 and 10.

Example

Mandy bought 10 pens.

She paid $2 for each pen.

How much did she pay altogether?

Story A

Look at the pictures on page 149.
Write multiplication stories.
Use multiplication tables of 5 and 10.

Story B

_____

_____

_____

_____

_____

Story C

_____

_____

_____

_____

_____

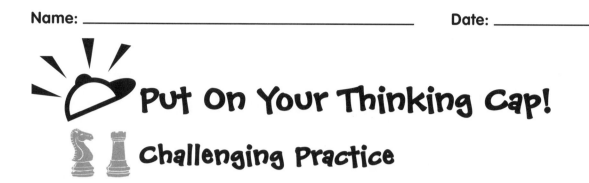

Put On Your Thinking Cap!

Challenging Practice

Fill in the blanks with the correct numbers.

Put On Your Thinking Cap!

Problem Solving

Solve.

A shop sells oranges and apples packed as shown.

bag of
10 oranges

bag of
5 apples

For every 10 oranges Jennifer buys, she also buys 5 apples.
She buys 20 oranges.
How many bags of fruits does she buy altogether?

You may want to
draw a diagram to
help you.

Jennifer buys _____ bags of fruits altogether.

Chapter Review/Test

Vocabulary
Fill in the blanks.
Circle the words that belong.

1.   15, _____, 25, 30, _____, 40

   To find the answer, (multiply / skip-count) by fives.

2. $\boxed{5 \times 2 = 10}$ $\boxed{2 \times 5 = 10}$

   These are (addition facts / related multiplication facts).

Concepts and Skills
Use dot paper to find the missing numbers.

3.   4.

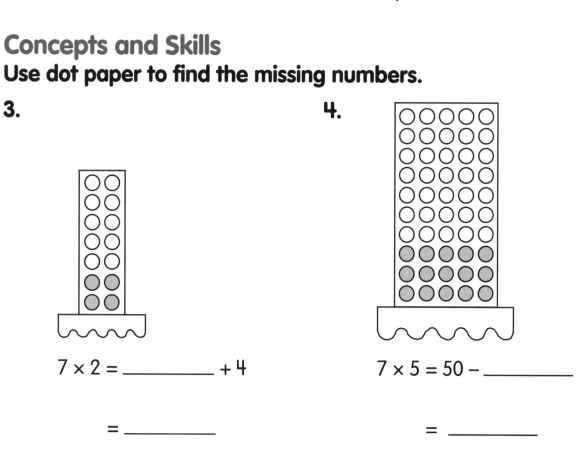

   $7 \times 2 = $ _____ $+ 4$ $7 \times 5 = 50 - $ _____

   $= $ _____ $= $ _____

Use dot paper to find the missing numbers.

5.

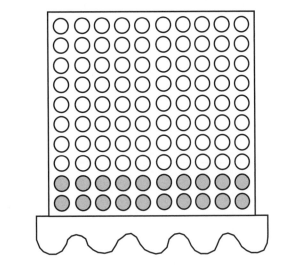

$$8 \times 10 = 100 - \underline{\hspace{2cm}}$$

$$= \underline{\hspace{2cm}}$$

6. $5 \times 2 = \underline{\hspace{2cm}}$

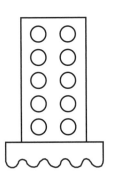

$2 \times 5 = \underline{\hspace{2cm}}$

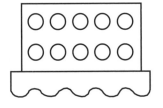

7. $4 \times 5 = \underline{\hspace{2cm}}$

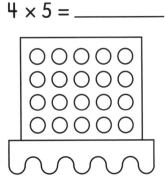

$5 \times 4 = \underline{\hspace{2cm}}$

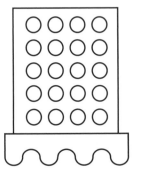

Name: _____   Date: _____

Use dot paper to find the missing numbers.

8. $7 \times 10 =$ _____ $10 \times 7 =$ _____

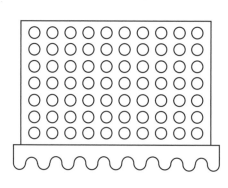   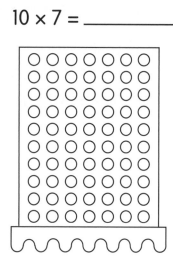

Find the missing numbers.
Then match the numbers to the letters to answer the riddle.

9.

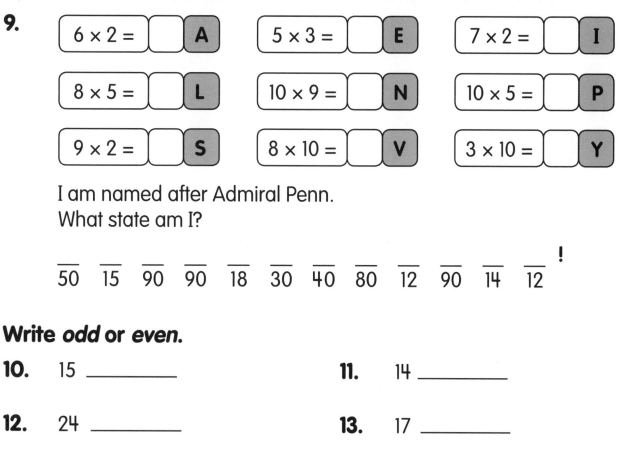

$6 \times 2 =$ ☐ **A**	$5 \times 3 =$ ☐ **E**	$7 \times 2 =$ ☐ **I**
$8 \times 5 =$ ☐ **L**	$10 \times 9 =$ ☐ **N**	$10 \times 5 =$ ☐ **P**
$9 \times 2 =$ ☐ **S**	$8 \times 10 =$ ☐ **V**	$3 \times 10 =$ ☐ **Y**

I am named after Admiral Penn.
What state am I?

$\overline{50}$ $\overline{15}$ $\overline{90}$ $\overline{90}$ $\overline{18}$ $\overline{30}$ $\overline{40}$ $\overline{80}$ $\overline{12}$ $\overline{90}$ $\overline{14}$ $\overline{12}$ **!**

Write *odd* or *even*.

10.   15 _____   **11.**   14 _____

12.   24 _____   **13.**   17 _____

Problem Solving
Use skip-counting or dot paper to solve.

14. Teddy grills 8 skewers of chicken.
Each skewer has 2 pieces of chicken.
How many pieces of chicken does he grill?

He grills _____ pieces of chicken.

15. Mr. Wilson has some strawberries.
He gives an equal number of strawberries to 10 children.
Each child gets 6 strawberries.
How many strawberries does Mr. Wilson have?

Mr. Wilson has _____ strawberries.

16. Jess has 4 friends.
She gives each friend 5 pennies.
How many pennies did Jess give away?

Jess gives away _____ pennies.

Cumulative Review

for Chapters 5 and 6

Concepts and Skills

Draw ☺.

1. Draw 4 groups of 3 ☺.

2. Draw 3 groups of 4 ☺.

Find the missing numbers.

3. $2 + 2 + 2 + 2 + 2 + 2 = $ _____ $\times 2$

4. $3 + 3 + 3 + 3 + 3$ is _____ groups of _____.

5.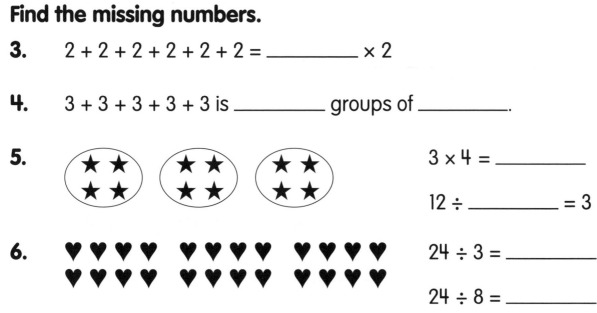

$3 \times 4 = $ _____

$12 \div $ _____ $= 3$

6.

$24 \div 3 = $ _____

$24 \div 8 = $ _____

Find the missing numbers.

7. Divide 20 socks so there are 5 socks in each group.

Subtract groups of 5 until there is nothing left.

20 – _____ – _____ – _____ – _____ = _____

Groups of five are subtracted _____ times.

20 ÷ 5 = _____

Cross out what does not belong.

8.

	7 groups of 5
5 + 5 + 5 + 5 + 5 + 5 + 5	5 sevens

9.

	Subtract groups of three 2 times.
6 – 2 – 2 – 2 = 0	6 ÷ 2 = 3

Fill in the blanks.

10. Divide 16 fruit bars equally on 4 trays.

16 ÷ _____ = _____

There are _____ fruit bars on each tray.

11. 6 bugs are on each of the 3 branches.

6 × _____ = _____

There are _____ bugs altogether.

12. Divide 20 crayons equally among 5 children.

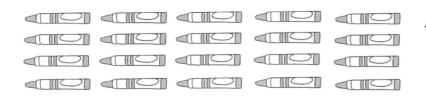 

20 ÷ _____ = _____

Each child gets _____ crayons.

Skip-count.

13. 2, 4, 6, _____, _____, _____, _____, _____, _____, _____

14. 5, 10, 15, _____, _____, _____, _____, _____, _____, _____

15. 10, 20, 30, _____, _____, _____, _____, _____, _____, _____

Fill in the blanks.

16. 2 groups of 2 = _____ × _____ = _____

17. 5 groups of 2 = _____ × _____ = _____

18. 6 groups of 5 = _____ × _____ = _____

19. 7 groups of 5 = _____ × _____ = _____

Use the dot paper to find the missing numbers.

20.

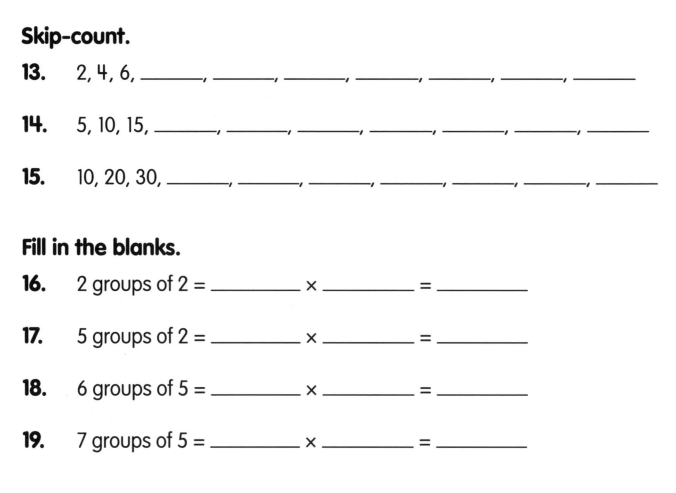

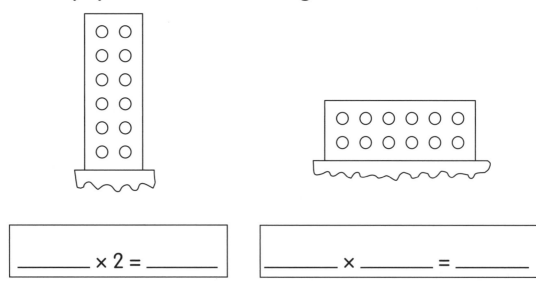

_____ × 2 = _____   _____ × _____ = _____

21.

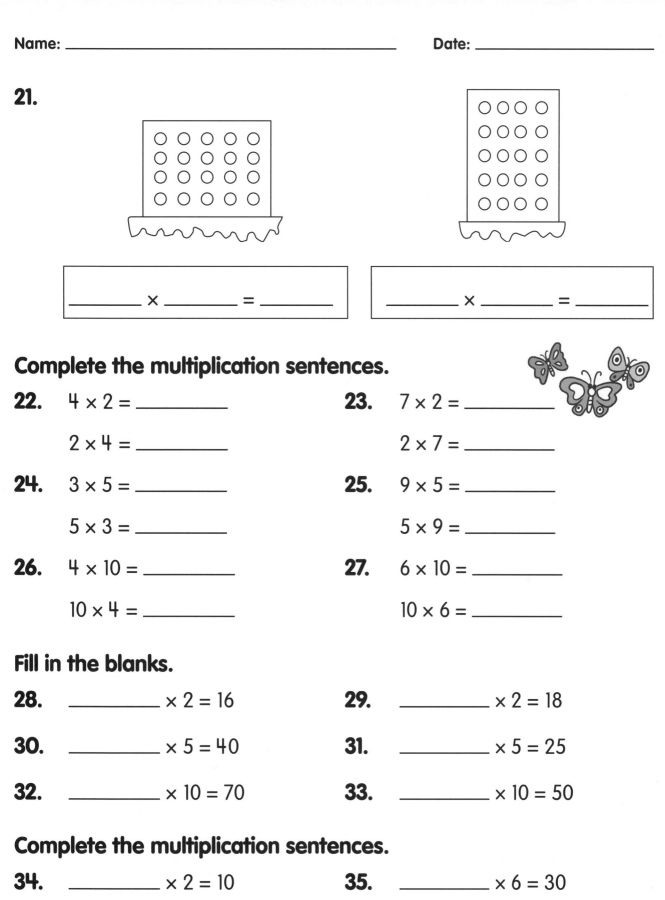

_____ × _____ = _____   _____ × _____ = _____

Complete the multiplication sentences.

22. 4 × 2 = _____

2 × 4 = _____

23. 7 × 2 = _____

2 × 7 = _____

24. 3 × 5 = _____

5 × 3 = _____

25. 9 × 5 = _____

5 × 9 = _____

26. 4 × 10 = _____

10 × 4 = _____

27. 6 × 10 = _____

10 × 6 = _____

Fill in the blanks.

28. _____ × 2 = 16

29. _____ × 2 = 18

30. _____ × 5 = 40

31. _____ × 5 = 25

32. _____ × 10 = 70

33. _____ × 10 = 50

Complete the multiplication sentences.

34. _____ × 2 = 10

35. _____ × 6 = 30

36. _____ × 10 = 20

37. _____ × 10 = 70

Problem Solving

Solve.

38. A grocer sells 5 oranges in a bag.
Mr. Diaz buys 6 bags of oranges.
How many oranges does he buy in all?

He buys _____ oranges in all.

39. Shauna puts some chairs in rows of 9.
There are 2 rows of chairs.
How many chairs are there?

There are _____ chairs.

40. Ling's Travel has 10 new alarm clocks.
Each clock needs 4 batteries.
How many batteries are needed in all?

_____ batteries are needed in all.

41. There are 18 seashells.
They are divided into 2 equal groups.
How many seashells are in each group?

_____ seashells are in each group.

42. Mr. Jenkins spends $30 on books.
Each book costs $10.
How many books does Mr. Jenkins buy?

Mr. Jenkins buys _____ books.

43. The school chef has 30 mini-pizzas.
She divides them equally among a few children.
  a. If each child gets 5 mini-pizzas, how many children are there?
  b. If there are 10 children, how many mini-pizzas will each child get?

  a. There are _____ children.

  b. Each child will get _____ mini-pizzas.

Metric Measurement of Length

CHAPTER 7

Practice 1   Measuring in Meters

Look at the pictures.
Fill in the blanks with *more* or *less*.

1.

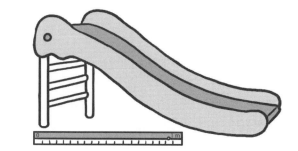

The length of the rope is _____ than 1 meter.

2.

The length of the slide is _____ than 1 meter.

3.

The height of the bookcase is

_____ than 1 meter.

Fill in the blanks.

4. Metersticks are placed against two boxes.

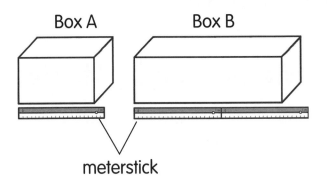

meterstick

a. Which box is about 1 meter long? Box _____

Fill in the blanks with *more* or *less*.

b. Box A is _____ than 1 meter long.

c. Box B is _____ than 1 meter long.

5. Metersticks are placed against a board.

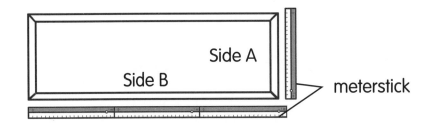

Side A

Side B

meterstick

a. Which side of the board is about 3 meters long?

Side _____

b. Side A is shorter than _____ meter.

c. Side B is shorter than _____ meters.

Name: _____   Date: _____

Look at the list below.

Check (✔) the columns that are true.

You will need a meterstick or a 1-meter string to measure some items.

6.

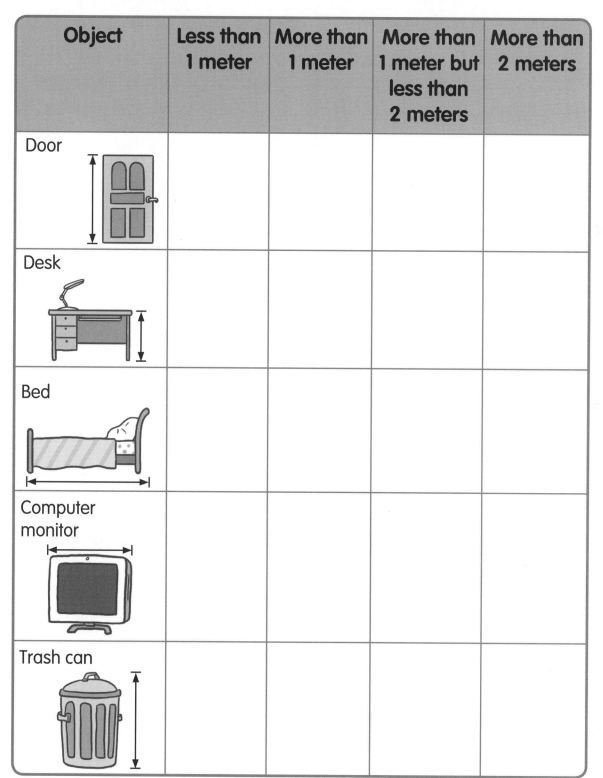

Object	Less than 1 meter	More than 1 meter	More than 1 meter but less than 2 meters	More than 2 meters
Door				
Desk				
Bed				
Computer monitor				
Trash can				

Name three objects that match each length.

7.

Length	Object
Less than 1 meter long	
About 1 meter long	
More than 1 meter long	

Fill in the blanks.
Use string and a meterstick.

8.   Mark on the string with a pencil how long you think 1 meter is.
      Then use a meterstick to measure this length.
      Did you mark more or less than 1 meter on your string?

      _____

9.   Next, mark on the string how long you think 2 meters are.
      Then use a meterstick to measure this length.
      Did you mark more or less than 2 meters on your string?

      _____

Practice 2   Comparing Lengths in Meters

Fill in the blanks.

1.   Look at the two ropes.

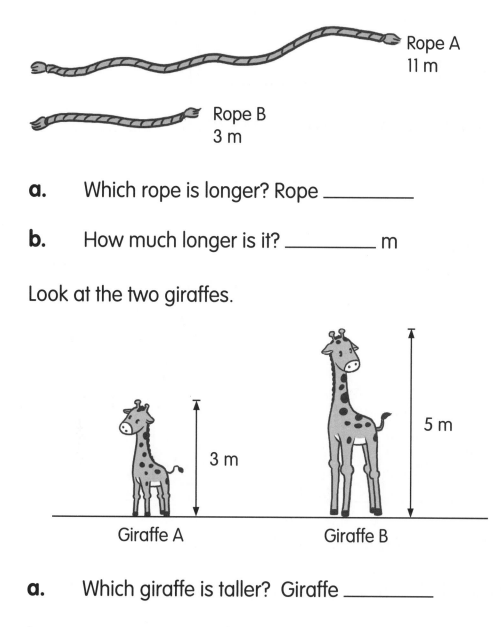

Rope A
11 m

Rope B
3 m

a.   Which rope is longer? Rope _____

b.   How much longer is it? _____ m

2.   Look at the two giraffes.

3 m

5 m

Giraffe A   Giraffe B

a.   Which giraffe is taller? Giraffe _____

b.   How much taller is it? _____ m

3. Look at the sides of the rectangle.

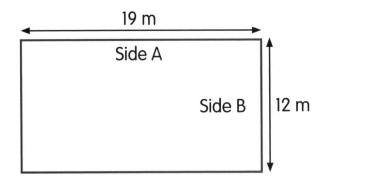

19 m

Side A

Side B 12 m

a. Which is shorter, Side A or Side B? Side _____

b. How much shorter is it? _____ m

4. Look at the buildings.

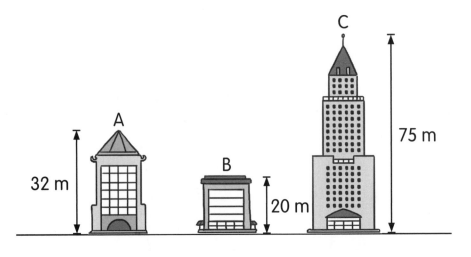

C

A

32 m

B

20 m

75 m

a. Which building is the shortest? Building _____

b. Which building is the tallest? Building _____

c. Building B is _____ meters shorter than Building C.

d. How much taller is Building C than Building A? _____ m

Practice 3   Measuring in Centimeters

**Check (✔) the correct way to measure
the length of the pencil.**

1.

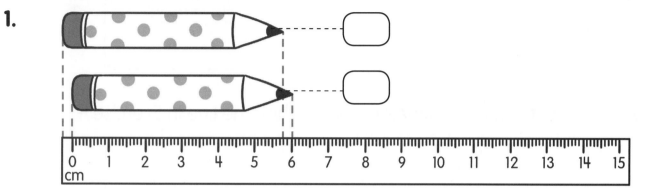

Use your centimeter ruler to draw.

2.   A line that is 5 centimeters long

3.   A line that is 12 centimeters long

4.   A line that is 9 centimeters long

Use your centimeter ruler to draw.

5. A line that is 6 centimeters long

6. A line that is 2 centimeters shorter than the line in Exercise 4.

7. A line that is 2 centimeters longer than the line in Exercise 5.

Use a piece of string to find the length.

8.

_____ cm

9.

_____ cm

10.

_____ cm

Cut a piece of string as long as the drawing below.
Then place the string on a centimeter ruler to find its length.

11.   **a.** How long is the string? _____ cm

string

b. This string is used to form the following shapes.
Use a string and a centimeter ruler to measure each of them.

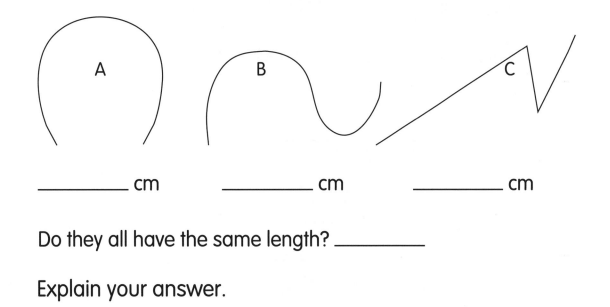

_____ cm   _____ cm   _____ cm

Do they all have the same length? _____

Explain your answer.

_____

_____

Find the missing numbers.

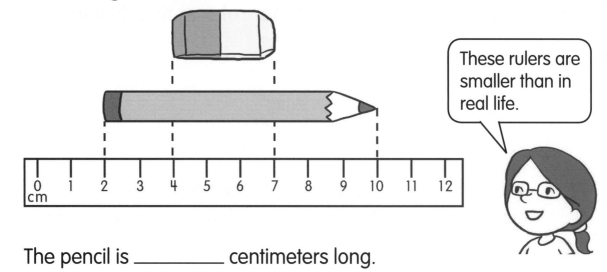

These rulers are smaller than in real life.

12. The pencil is _____ centimeters long.

13. The eraser is _____ centimeters long.

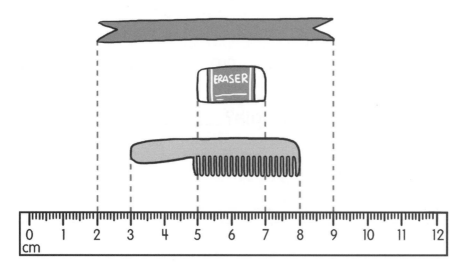

14. The length of the comb is _____ centimeters.

15. The length of the ribbon is _____ centimeters.

16. The length of the eraser is _____ centimeters.

© Marshall Cavendish International (Singapore) Private Limited.

Practice 4   Comparing Lengths in Centimeters

Look at each drawing.
Then fill in the blanks.

1.

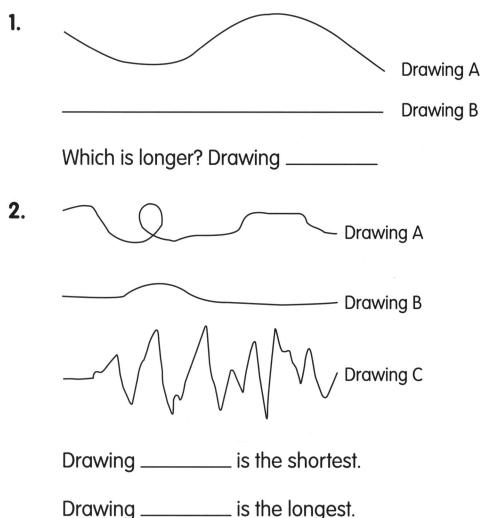

Drawing A

Drawing B

Which is longer? Drawing _____

2.

Drawing A

Drawing B

Drawing C

Drawing _____ is the shortest.

Drawing _____ is the longest.

Explain your answers.

_____

_____

_____

_____

Find each length.

3.

The straw is about ＿＿＿＿＿ centimeters long.

4.

The wallet is about ＿＿＿＿＿ centimeters long.

5.

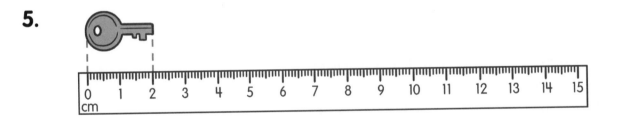

The key is about ＿＿＿＿＿ centimeters long.

These rulers are smaller than in real life.

Find each length.

6.

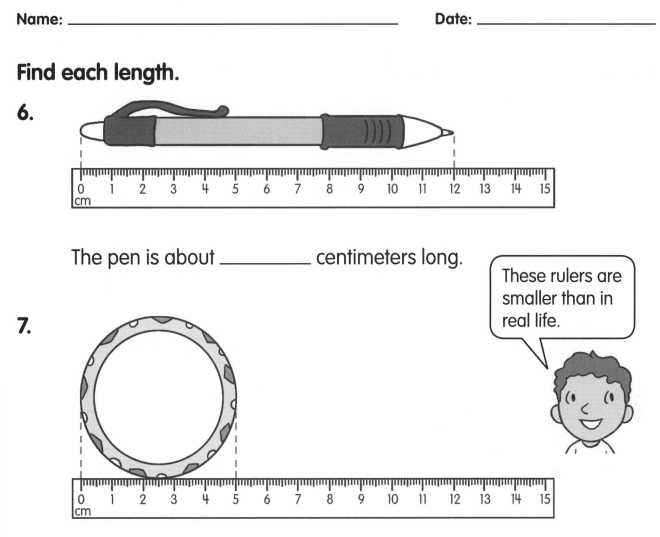

The pen is about _____ centimeters long.

These rulers are smaller than in real life.

7.

The bracelet is about _____ centimeters wide.

Use your answers for Exercises 3 to 6.
Fill in the blanks with *longer* or *shorter*.

8.   The pen is _____ than the straw.

9.   The key is _____ than the pen.

10.   The wallet is _____ than the straw.

Use your answers for Exercises 3 to 7.
Fill in the blanks.

11.   The straw is _____ centimeters longer than the key.

12.   The straw is _____ centimeters shorter than the pen.

13.   The pen is _____ centimeters longer than the key.

14.   The bracelet is _____ centimeter shorter than the wallet.

15.   The longest object is the _____.

16.   The shortest object is the _____.

Practice 5 Real-World Problems: Metric Length

Solve.

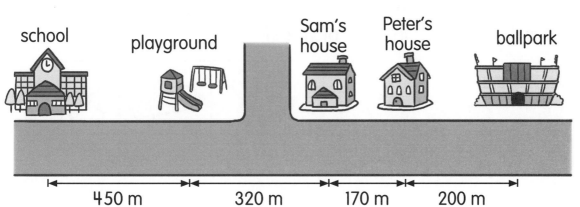

1. How far does Sam walk from his house to the playground? _____ m

2. How far is Peter's house from the playground? _____ m

3. Who lives nearer to the school, Sam or Peter? _____

4. How much nearer? _____ m

5. If Sam goes to the ballpark from his house, how far does he walk? _____ m

6. Peter left his house to walk to the ballpark.
   He has walked 123 meters.
   How much farther does he have to walk? _____ m

Solve.

7. There are two pictures.
One of them is 35 centimeters long.
The other is 86 centimeters long.
They are placed side by side.
What is the length of the two pictures?

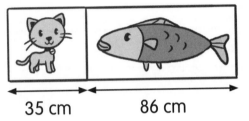

35 cm   86 cm

The length is _____ centimeters.

8. A ribbon is cut into three pieces.
They are 4 meters, 6 meters, and 2 meters long.
How long was the ribbon before it was cut?

The ribbon was _____ meters long.

9. Mrs. Chu has two pairs of chopsticks.
Each red chopstick is 19 centimeters long.
Each yellow chopstick is 22 centimeters long.

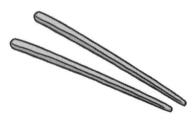

a. Which pair of chopsticks is longer?

The _____ chopsticks

b. How much longer? _____ cm

Solve.

10. A flag pole is 450 centimeters tall.
The top of the flag is 345 centimeters from the ground.
How much farther must it be raised to reach the top?

The flag must be raised _____

centimeters farther to reach the top.

11. The total length of two pieces of wood is 215 centimeters.
The first piece is 135 centimeters long.

a. What is the length of the second piece?

The length of the second piece is _____ centimeters.

b. How much shorter is the second piece than
the first piece?

The second piece is _____ centimeters shorter than
the first piece.

12. Max is 135 centimeters tall.
He is 18 centimeters taller than Rita.
Rita is 30 centimeters shorter than Jan.
How tall is Jan?

Jan is _____ centimeters tall.

13. Cody has a strip of paper 10 centimeters long.
He cuts it into three pieces.
One piece is 4 centimeters long.
The second piece is 3 centimeters long.
How long is the third piece of paper?

The third piece of paper is _____ centimeters long.

14. A string is 200 centimeters long.
Kaly uses 63 centimeters of it to tie a box.
She gives 48 centimeters of it to Susan.
How long is the string that Kaly has left?

The length of the string that Kaly has left is _____ centimeters.

© Marshall Cavendish International (Singapore) Private Limited.

Put On Your Thinking Cap!
Challenging Practice

Solve.

1. There are three drawings — A, B, and C.
    Drawing A is shown below.

    _____ Drawing A

    Drawing B is 2 centimeters longer than Drawing A.
    Drawing C is 3 centimeters shorter than Drawing B.
    How long is Drawing C?

2. Sara bought three pieces of ribbon.
    She bought 90 centimeters of ribbon in all.
    Check (✔) to show which three pieces of ribbon she bought.

Ribbon	Length of Ribbon	Check
A	25 cm	
B	42 cm	
C	38 cm	
D	15 cm	
E	10 cm	
F	20 cm	

Put On Your Thinking Cap!

Problem Solving

The picture shows the shadows of two trees.

Tree A
?

Tree B
?

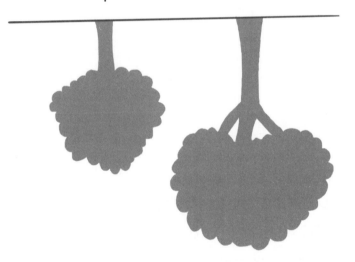

Look at the shadows. Which tree is taller? Tree _____

Explain your answer.

_____

_____

_____

Chapter Review/Test
Vocabulary
Fill in the blanks with words from the box.

| meters | meterstick | height | centimeters | width | length |

1.

To find how high this bookcase is, I need to find its _____.

2. An earthworm is about 10 _____ long.

3.

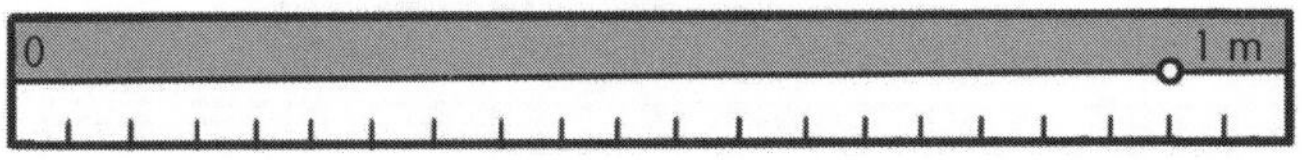

This is a _____.

Fill in the blanks with words from the box.

| meters | meterstick | height | centimeters | width | length |

4.

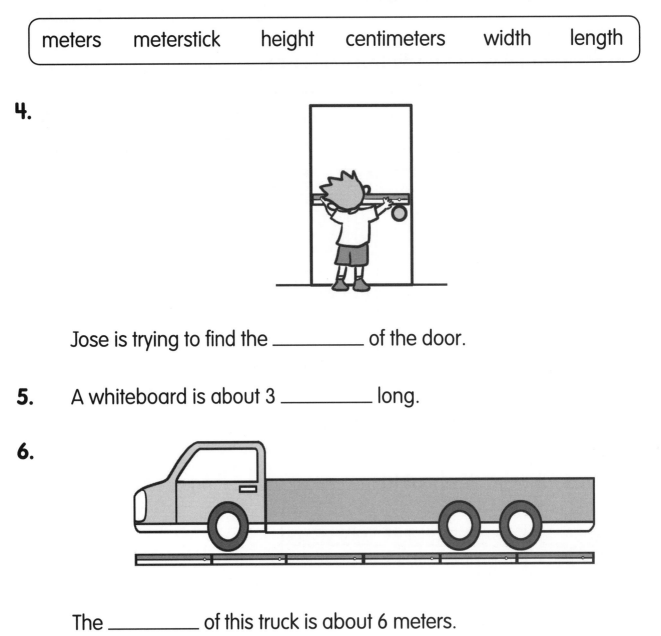

Jose is trying to find the _____ of the door.

5. A whiteboard is about 3 _____ long.

6.

The _____ of this truck is about 6 meters.

Concepts and Skills
Check (✔) the correct answers.

7.   What is the length of your math textbook?

Length	Check
About 1 meter	
Less than 1 meter	
More than 1 meter	

8.   What is the height of your desk?

Height	Check
About 1 meter	
Less than 1 meter	
More than 8 meters	
Less than 3 meters	

9.   What is the height of your classroom?

Height	Check
About 1 meter	
Less than 1 meter	
More than 8 meters	
Less than 8 meters	

Look at the objects measured.
Then fill in the blanks.

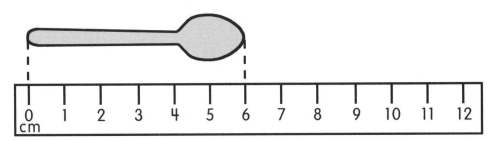

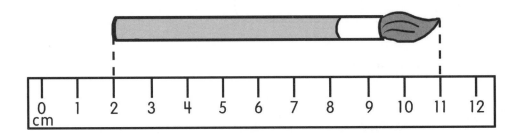

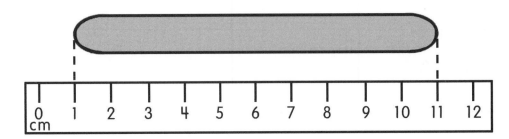

What are the lengths of the

10. spoon: _____ cm

11. brush: _____ cm

12. craftstick: _____ cm

13. The craftstick is _____ centimeters longer than the spoon.

14. The _____ is the shortest.

Solve.

15.   Shane has 5 meters of cloth.
He needs 16 meters more cloth to make some curtains.
How many meters of cloth are needed to make the curtains?

_____ meters of cloth are needed to make the curtains.

16.   Two boards are 26 meters long altogether.
One board is 8 meters long.
How long is the other board?

The other board is _____ meters long.

17. Bella is 161 centimeters tall.
She is 12 centimeters taller than Joshua.
How tall is Joshua?

Joshua is _____ centimeters tall.

18. Raul has a box that is 9 centimeters wide.
Ling's box is 3 centimeters wider than Raul's box.
Will both their boxes fit on a shelf that is 30 centimeters wide?
Explain why.

_____

_____

_____

_____

_____

_____

CHAPTER 8 Mass

Practice 1   Measuring in Kilograms

Fill in the blanks.

| more than | less than | as heavy as | package | squash | pear |

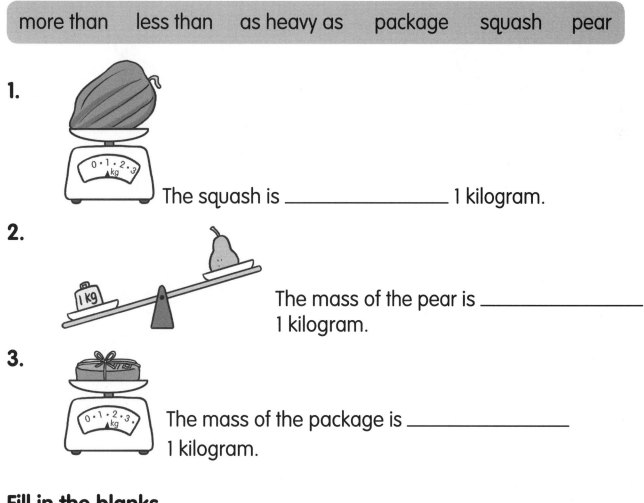

1.

The squash is _____ 1 kilogram.

2.

The mass of the pear is _____ 1 kilogram.

3.

The mass of the package is _____ 1 kilogram.

Fill in the blanks.
Use your answers in Exercises 1 to 3 to help you.

4.   The _____ is the lightest.

5.   The _____ is the heaviest.

Read each scale.
Then write the mass.

6.

_____ kg

7.

_____ kg

8.

_____ kg

9.

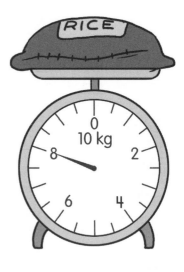

_____ kg

Practice 2 Comparing Masses in Kilograms

Look at the pictures.
Then fill in the blanks.

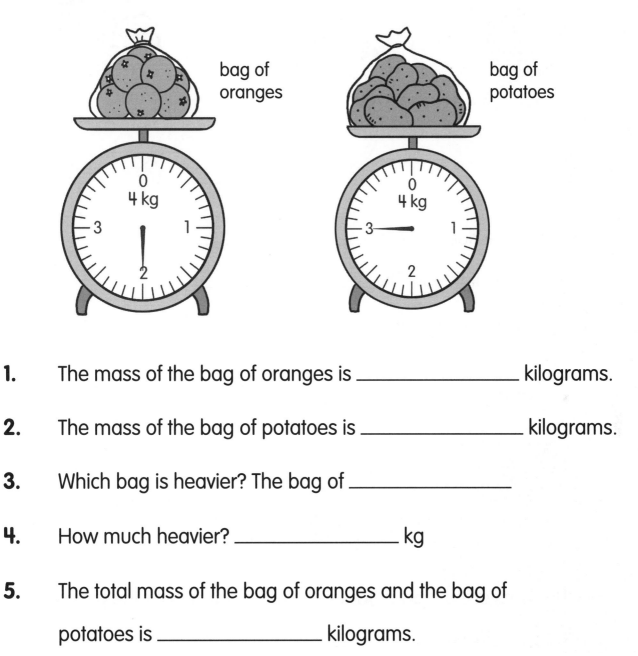

bag of
oranges

bag of
potatoes

1. The mass of the bag of oranges is _____ kilograms.

2. The mass of the bag of potatoes is _____ kilograms.

3. Which bag is heavier? The bag of _____

4. How much heavier? _____ kg

5. The total mass of the bag of oranges and the bag of

potatoes is _____ kilograms.

**Look at the pictures.
Then answer the questions.**

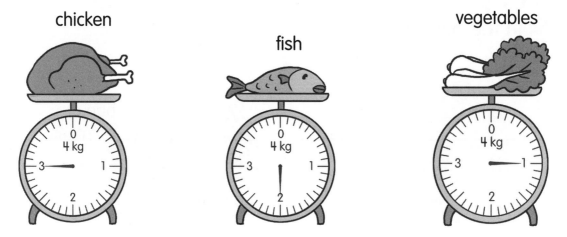

chicken

fish

vegetables

6.   Which is the heaviest? The _____

7.   Which is the lightest? The _____

8.   Order the items from lightest to heaviest.

   _____, _____, _____
        lightest   heaviest

9.

If the items are put on a balance scale, do you think the picture

above is correct? _____

Why or why not? _____

_____

_____

Fill in the blanks.

The pictures show Ally's and Roger's mass.

Ally

Roger

10. Ally has a mass of _____ kilograms.

11. Roger has a mass of _____ kilograms.

12. Who is heavier, Roger or Ally? _____

13. How much heavier? _____ kg

14. What is the total mass of Roger and Ally?

_____ kg

Read each sentence.
Write *True* or *False*.

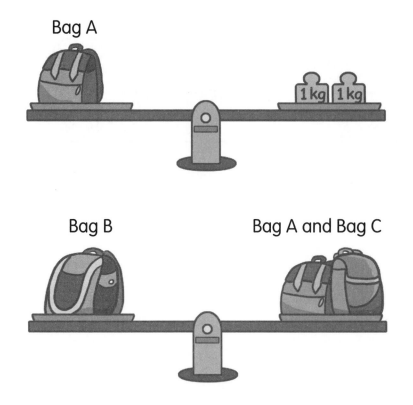

Bag A

1 kg 1 kg

Bag B   Bag A and Bag C

15. The mass of Bag A is 2 kilograms. _____

16. Bag B has the same mass as the total mass of both

Bag A and Bag C. _____

17. The mass of Bag A is different from the mass of Bag B.

_____

18. Bag B is heavier than Bag C. _____

Practice 3   Measuring in Grams

Fill in the blanks.
The mass of each 1g is 1 gram.

1.

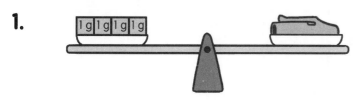

The cap of a pen has a mass of _____ grams.

2.

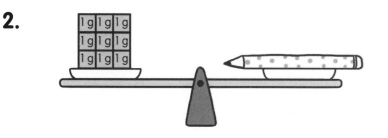

The pencil has a mass of _____ grams.

3.

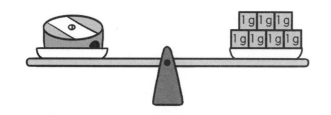

The sharpener has a mass of _____ grams.

4.

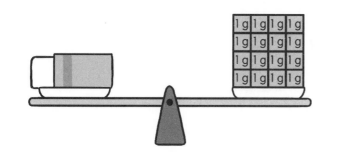

The eraser has a mass of _____ grams.

Fill in the missing numbers.

5.

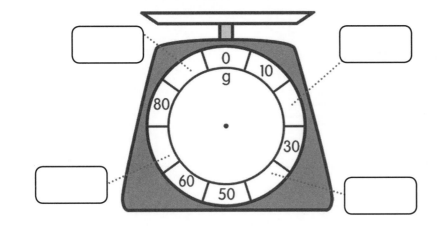

6.

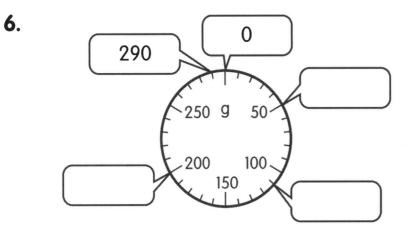

7.

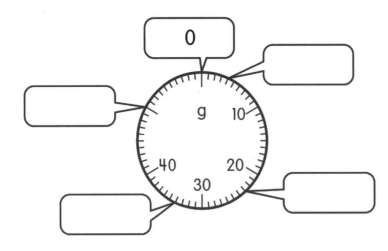

Fill in the missing numbers.

8.

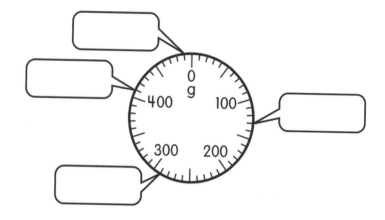

Fill in the blanks.

9.

The sandwich has

a mass of _____ grams.

10.

The lunch box has

a mass of _____ grams.

Fill in the blanks.

11.

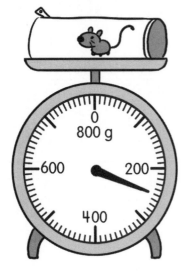

The pencil case has a mass of _____ grams.

12.

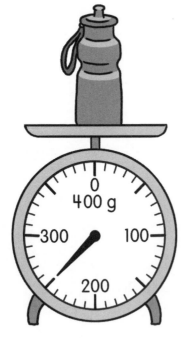

The water bottle has a mass of _____ grams.

Fill in the blanks.

13.

The bag of peanuts has a mass of _____ grams.

14.

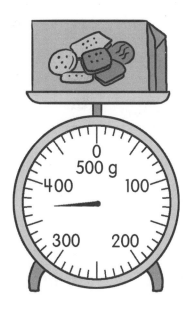

The box of crackers has a mass of _____ grams.

Fill in the blanks.

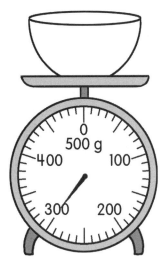

15. The empty bowl has a mass of _____ grams.

16. Some marbles are put into the bowl.

The bowl and the marbles have a mass of _____ grams.

17. What is the mass of the marbles? _____ grams

Practice 4 Comparing Masses in Grams

Find the mass of each vegetable.
Then fill in the blanks.

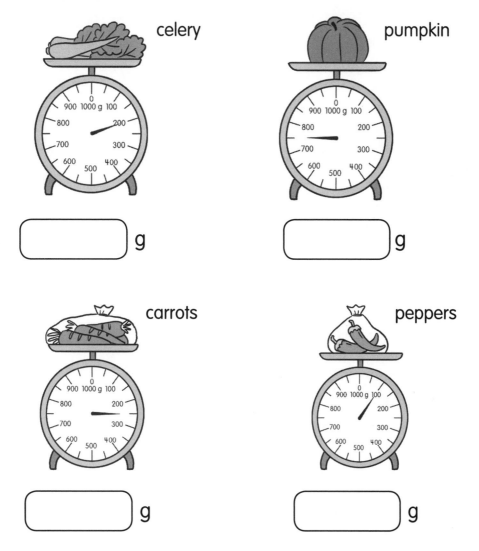

celery

[_____] g

pumpkin

[_____] g

carrots

[_____] g

peppers

[_____] g

1. The _____ is the heaviest.

2. The _____ are the lightest.

3. The pumpkin is _____ grams heavier than the celery.

4. The _____ is heavier than the bag of peppers
    but lighter than the bag of carrots.

Look at the boxes.
Then fill in the blanks.

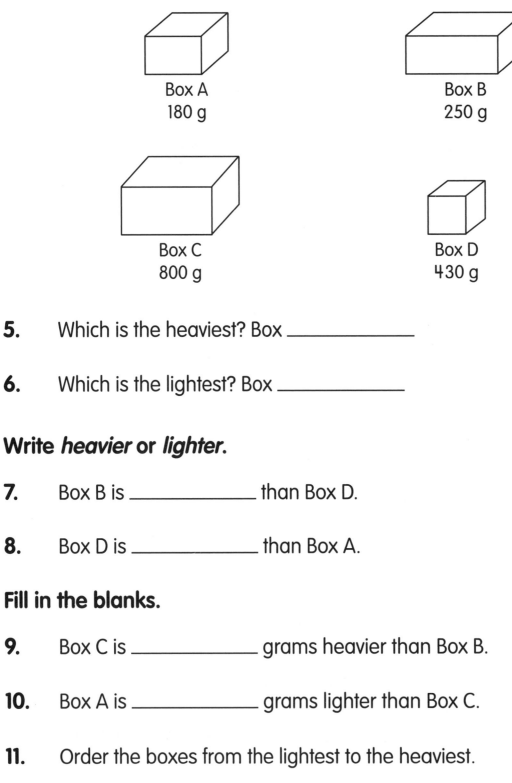

Box A
180 g

Box B
250 g

Box C
800 g

Box D
430 g

5. Which is the heaviest? Box _____

6. Which is the lightest? Box _____

Write *heavier* or *lighter*.

7. Box B is _____ than Box D.

8. Box D is _____ than Box A.

Fill in the blanks.

9. Box C is _____ grams heavier than Box B.

10. Box A is _____ grams lighter than Box C.

11. Order the boxes from the lightest to the heaviest.

_____, _____, _____, _____
lightest   heaviest

Practice 5 Real-World Problems: Mass

Solve.
Use bar models to help you.

1. Angelina has two dogs.
The masses of the two dogs are 35 kilograms
and 67 kilograms.
What is the total mass of the two dogs?

The total mass of the two dogs is _____ kilograms.

2. Miguel has a mass of 32 kilograms.
He is 5 kilograms lighter than Sal.
What is Sal's mass?

Sal's mass is _____ kilograms.

3. Mr. Souza needs 400 grams of clay to make a small statue.
He has only 143 grams of clay.
How much more clay does he need?

He needs _____ grams more clay.

Solve.

4. Ali has a mass of 25 kilograms.
   Tyrone is 6 kilograms heavier than Ali.
   What is their total mass?

   Their total mass is _____ kilograms.

5. Twyla buys a bag of onions with a mass of 750 grams.
   She uses 100 grams of the onions for lunch.
   She uses 480 grams of the onions for dinner.
   What is the mass of the onions that are left?

   The mass of onions left is _____ grams.

6. Tim sells 45 kilograms of rice on Monday.
   He sells 18 kilograms less rice on Tuesday than on Monday.
   How much rice does he sell in all on the two days?

   He sells _____ kilograms of rice in all on the two days.

Math Journal

Look at the pictures.

1. Write sentences to compare the mass of the boxes.
Use the words *lighter, heavier, lightest,* and *heaviest.*

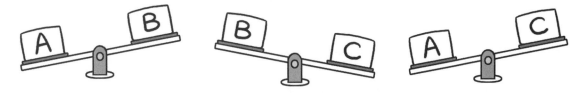

_____

_____

_____

_____

_____

_____

2. Order the boxes from heaviest to lightest.

_____, _____, _____
heaviest   lightest

Write *True* or *False*.

Example

The stapler is as heavy as the pen.

False

---

3. The pen has a mass of 60 grams.

    _____

4. The stapler is 70 grams lighter than the pen.

    _____

5. The book is the heaviest.

    _____

6. The total mass of the stapler and the pen is 190 grams.

    _____

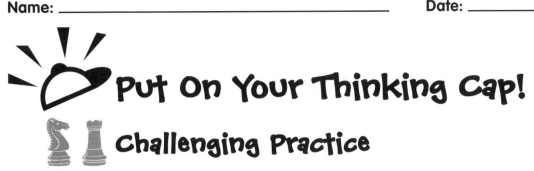

Put On Your Thinking Cap!

Challenging Practice

Fill in the blanks.

1. In Picture A, 3 100 g are needed to make the needle on the scale point as shown.
   How many 100 g are needed to make the needle point as shown in Picture B?

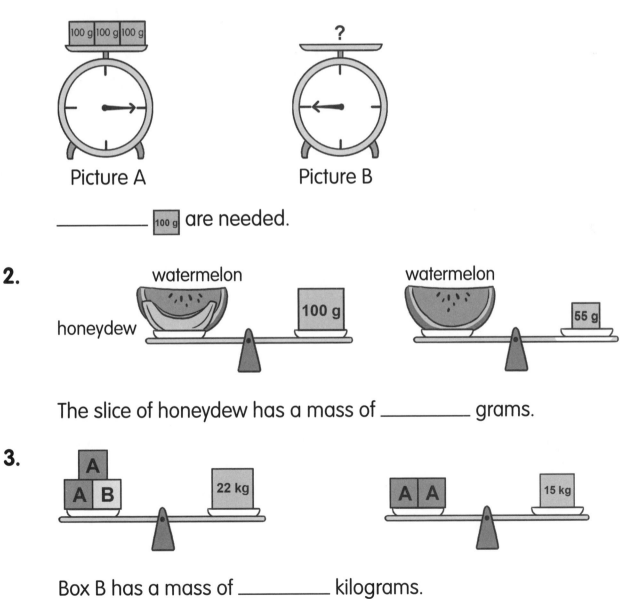

Picture A   Picture B

_____ 100 g are needed.

2.
watermelon   watermelon

honeydew   100 g   55 g

The slice of honeydew has a mass of _____ grams.

3.

A   22 kg   A A   15 kg
A B

Box B has a mass of _____ kilograms.

Put On Your Thinking Cap!

Problem Solving

Solve.

Draw a model to help you.

a. What is the mass of one ball? _____ g

b. What is the mass of the box? _____ g

Chapter Review/Test

Vocabulary

Fill in the blanks with words from the box.

> kilogram   heavier than   mass
> lightest   gram   measuring scale

1. A table is _____ a watch.

2. A _____ is a bigger unit of mass and a

    _____ is a smaller unit of mass.

3. To measure how heavy an object is, you find its _____.

4. You use a _____ to measure the mass of an object.

5.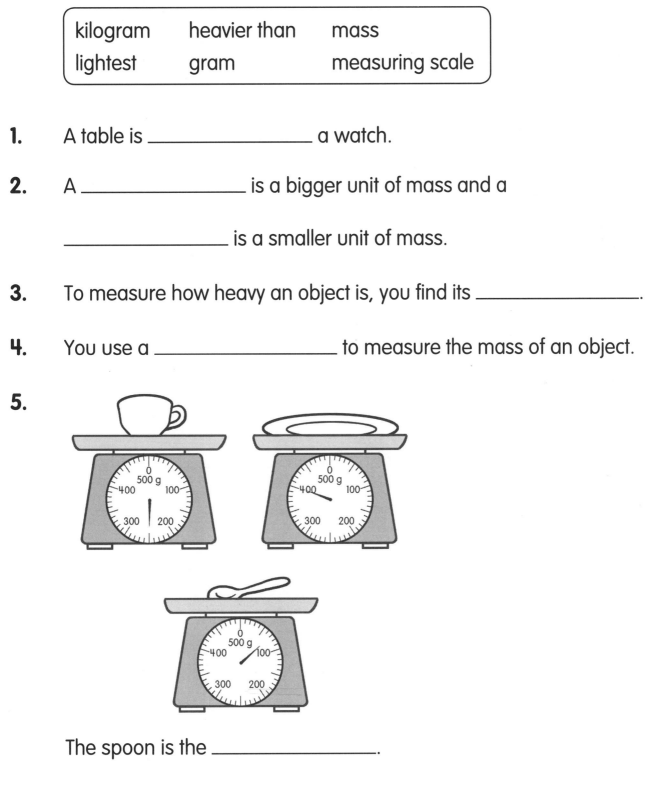

    The spoon is the _____.

Concepts and Skills
Answer the questions.

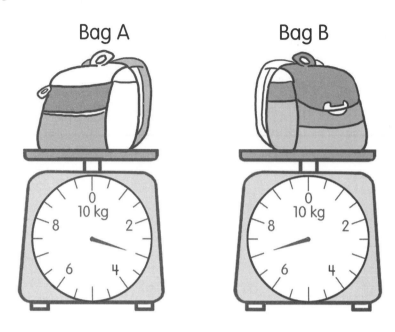

Bag A   Bag B

6. Which bag is heavier? Bag _____

7. How much heavier is it? _____ kg

8. What is the total mass of both bags? _____ kg

9. Which bottle is the lightest? Bottle _____

10. What is the difference in mass between the heaviest

and lightest bottle? _____ g

11. What is the total mass of Bottle A and Bottle C? _____ g

12. Order the bottles from lightest to heaviest.

_____, _____, _____
   lightest   heaviest

Problem Solving

Solve.

Use bar models to help you.

13. Mr. Shepherd has 5 kilograms of rice.
He buys another 8 kilograms of rice.
How many kilograms of rice does he have?

Mr. Shepherd has _____ kilograms of rice.

14. Claudia has two boxes.
The mass of Box A is 980 grams.
The mass of Box B is 750 grams.
What is the difference in masses between the two boxes?

The difference in masses between the two boxes is

_____ grams.

15.   Casey has 500 grams of carrots.
He buys another 400 grams of carrots.
He uses 725 grams of carrots for a recipe.
How many grams of carrots does he have left?

Casey has _____ grams of carrots left.

16.   Lily's dog weighs 27 kilograms.
Her dog is 2 kilograms heavier than Ben's dog.
Joe's dog is 5 kilograms heavier than Ben's dog.
What is the mass of Joe's dog?

The mass of Joe's dog is _____ kilograms.

17. A chef buys 45 kilograms of chicken.
He uses 7 kilograms of chicken on Tuesday.
He buys another 5 kilograms of chicken on Wednesday.
How many kilograms of chicken does he have left?

He has _____ kilograms of chicken left.

18. The mass of Nadia's pencil case is 87 grams.
The mass of Pete's pencil case is 12 grams more than
the mass of Nadia's pencil case.
The mass of Felix's pencil case is 10 grams less than
the mass of Pete's pencil case.
Find the mass of Felix's pencil case.

The mass of Felix's pencil case is _____ grams.

Volume

Practice 1   Getting to Know Volume

**Fill in the blanks with *more, less,* or *same.*

1.

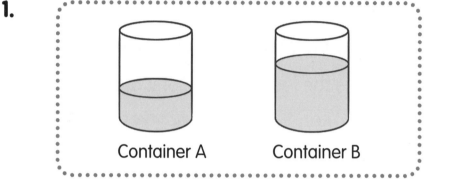

Container A   Container B

Container A and Container B are the same size.

a.   Container B has _____ water than Container A.

b.   Container A has _____ water than Container B.

2.

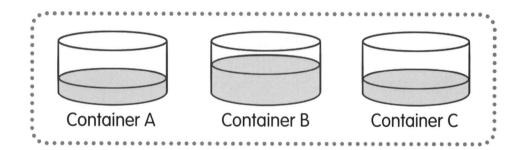

Container A   Container B   Container C

Container A, Container B, and Container C are the same size.

a.   Container A has _____ water than Container B.

b.   Container B has _____ water than Container A.

c.   Container A has the _____ amount of water as Container C.

Fill in the blanks.

3.

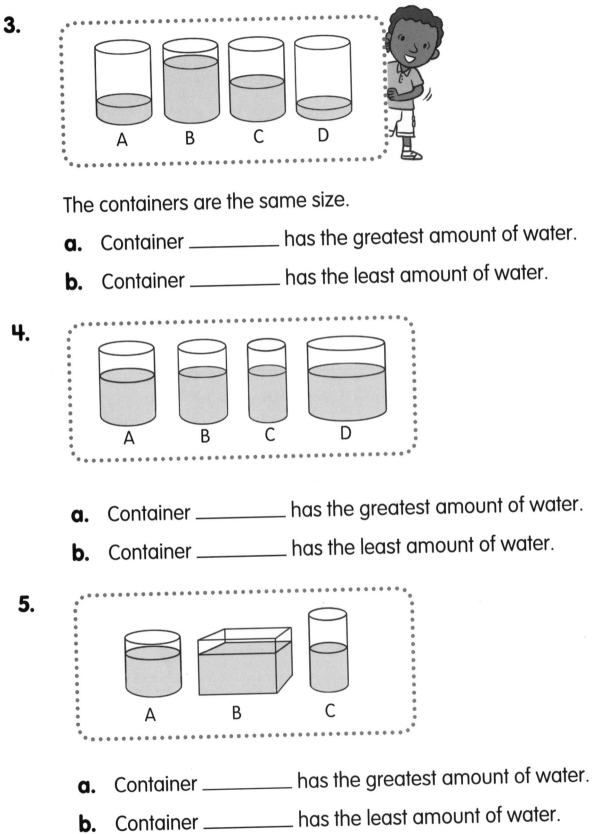

The containers are the same size.

a. Container _____ has the greatest amount of water.

b. Container _____ has the least amount of water.

4.

a. Container _____ has the greatest amount of water.

b. Container _____ has the least amount of water.

5.

a. Container _____ has the greatest amount of water.

b. Container _____ has the least amount of water.

Practice 2   Getting to Know Volume

Fill in the blanks.

Water is scooped out of a pail and poured into these containers.

Each is one scoop.

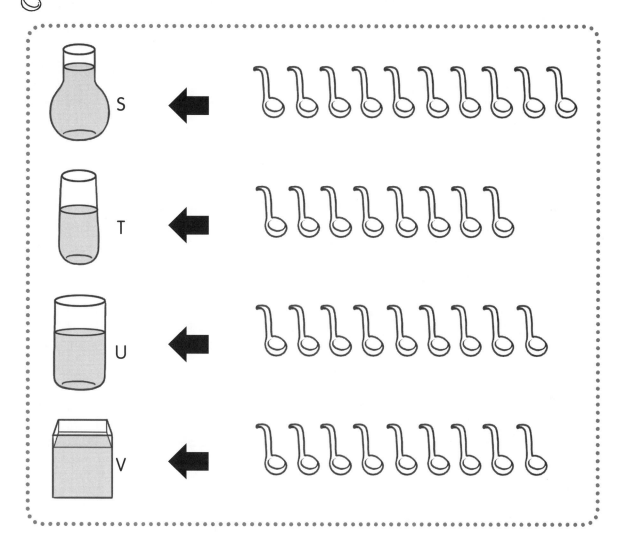

1. Container _____ has the greatest amount of water.

2. Container _____ has the least amount of water.

3. Containers _____ and _____ have the same amount of water.

4. Container _____ has more water than Container U.

5. Container V has more water than Container _____.

Fill in the blanks.

All the water in each container is used to fill the glasses.

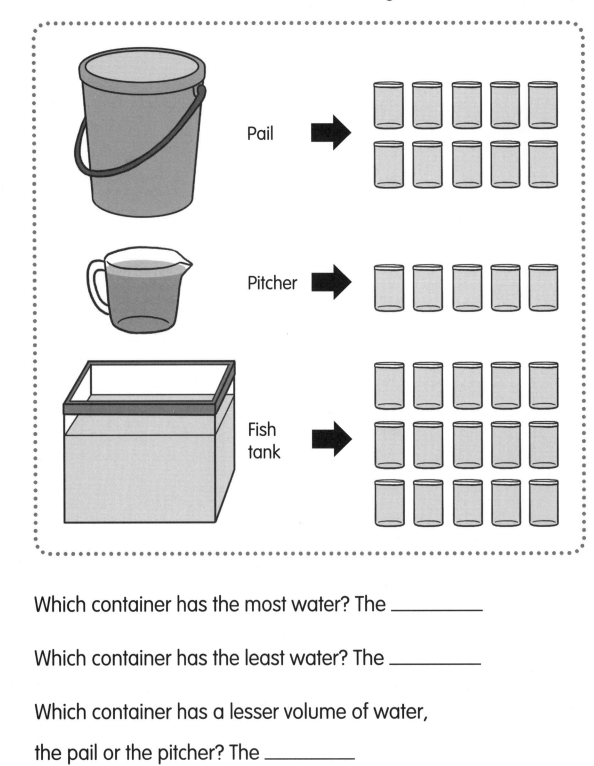

6. Which container has the most water? The _____

7. Which container has the least water? The _____

8. Which container has a lesser volume of water,

   the pail or the pitcher? The _____

Fill in the blanks.

Luisa fills glasses of the same size with all the water
from the pitcher, flask, and mug.

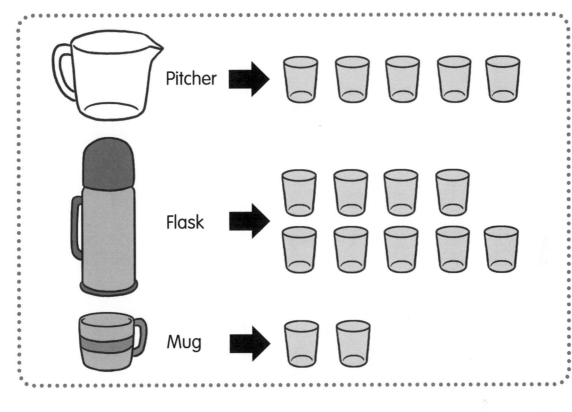

Pitcher

Flask

Mug

9.   The _____ has the most water.

10.   The _____ has the least water.

11.   There are _____ more glasses of water in the flask
than in the pitcher.

12.   There are _____ fewer glasses of water in the mug than
in the flask.

13.   Order the pitcher, flask, and mug.
Begin with the container that has the most water.

_____, _____, _____
     most   least

Fill in the blanks.

Brad fills glasses of the same size with all the water from
Kettle A, Kettle B, Kettle C, and Kettle D.

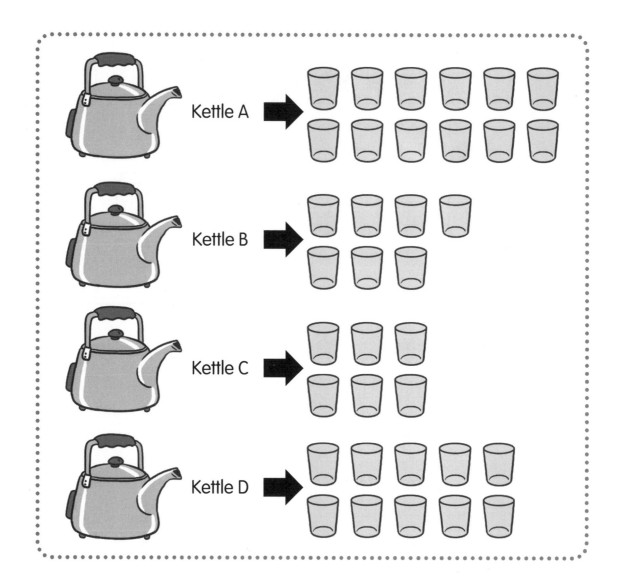

14. Kettle _____ has the most water.

15. Kettle _____ has the least water.

16. Kettle A has _____ more glasses of water than Kettle B.

17. Kettle C has 4 fewer glasses of water than Kettle _____.

Practice 3   Measuring in Liters

Find the volume of water in each container.

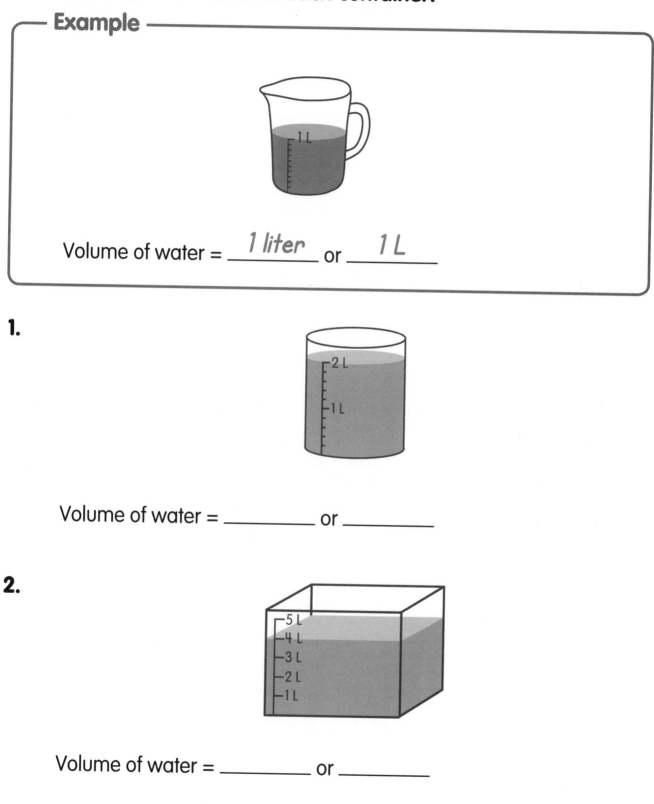

┌─ **Example** ───┐

Volume of water = ___*1 liter*___ or ___*1 L*___

└──┘

1.

Volume of water = _____ or _____

2.

Volume of water = _____ or _____

Find the volume of water in each container.

3.

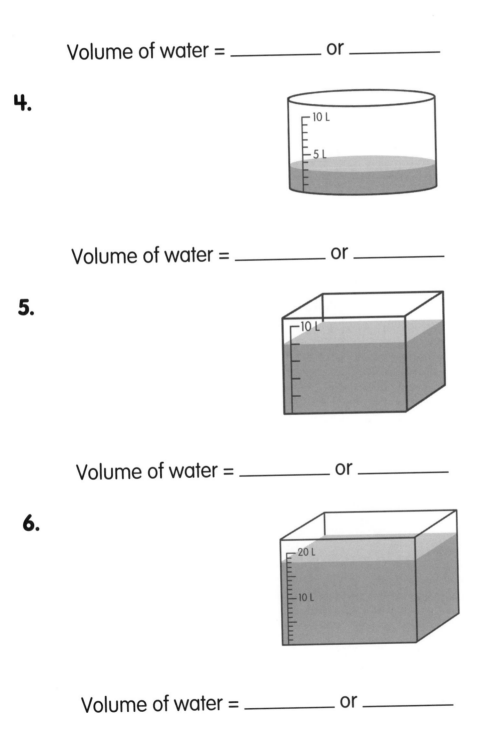

Volume of water = _____ or _____

4.

Volume of water = _____ or _____

5.

Volume of water = _____ or _____

6.

Volume of water = _____ or _____

Fill in the blanks.

7.

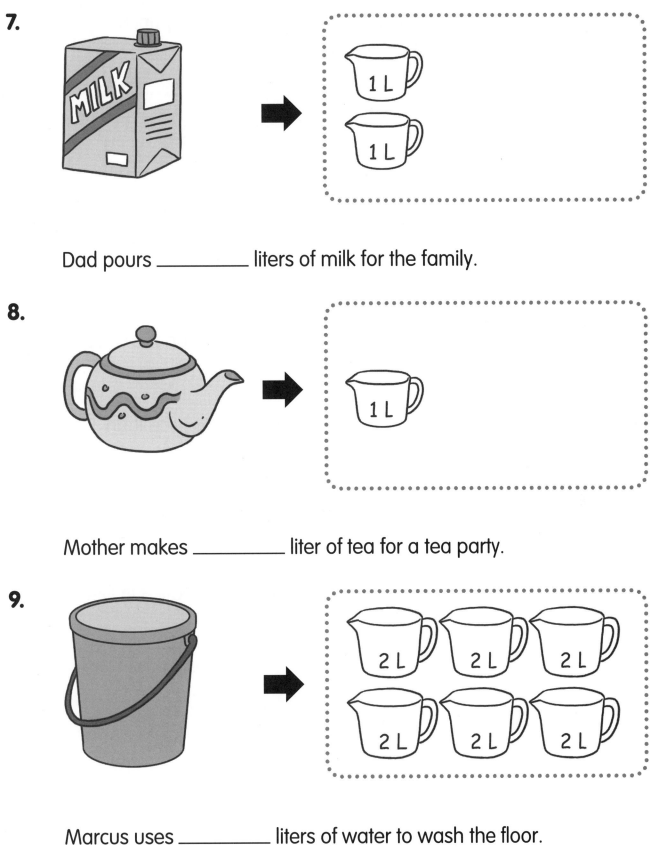

Dad pours _____ liters of milk for the family.

8.

Mother makes _____ liter of tea for a tea party.

9.

Marcus uses _____ liters of water to wash the floor.

Fill in the blanks.

10. Susan uses these volumes of juices to make fruit punch.
Write the volume of each juice.

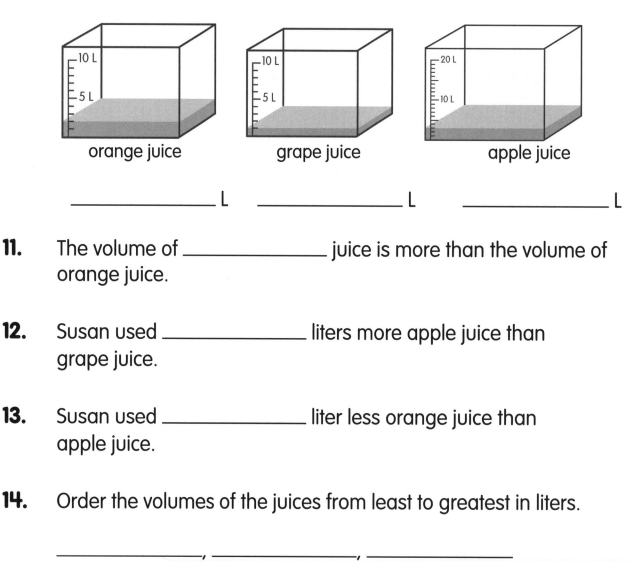

orange juice   grape juice   apple juice

_____ L   _____ L   _____ L

11. The volume of _____ juice is more than the volume of orange juice.

12. Susan used _____ liters more apple juice than grape juice.

13. Susan used _____ liter less orange juice than apple juice.

14. Order the volumes of the juices from least to greatest in liters.

_____, _____, _____
      least   greatest

Practice 4   Real-World Problems: Volume

Solve.
Use bar models to help you.

1.   Mrs. White brings 70 liters of juice to the school picnic.
After the picnic, 12 liters of juice are left.
How many liters of juice does everyone drink at the picnic?

They drink _____ liters of juice at the picnic.

2.   A fish tank contains 12 liters of water.
Another fish tank contains 7 liters of water.
What is the total volume of water in the two fish tanks?

The total volume of water in the two tanks is _____ liters.

Solve.
Use bar models to help you.

3. Sylvia fills two containers of the same size with water.
   She fills Container A with 5 liters of water.
   Then she fills Container B with 3 more liters of water
   than Container A.
   What is the total volume of water in both containers?

There are _____ liters of water in both containers.

4. A barrel has 60 liters of rainwater.
   Jan uses 17 liters to water her flower garden.
   She uses another 15 liters to water her vegetable garden.
   How much rainwater is left in the barrel?

There are _____ liters of rainwater left in the barrel.

Solve.
Use bar models to help you.

5.   Container A has 18 liters of water.
           Container B has 5 liters of water more than Container A.
           Container C has 16 liters of water less than Container B.
           What is the volume of water in Container C?

           There are _____ liters of water in Container C.

6.   Container A has 17 liters of water.
           It has 2 more liters of water than Container B
           Jasmine pours another 7 liters of water into Container B.
           What is the volume of water in Container B?

           There are _____ liters of water in Container B.

Math Journal

Read how Pete solved a real-world problem.

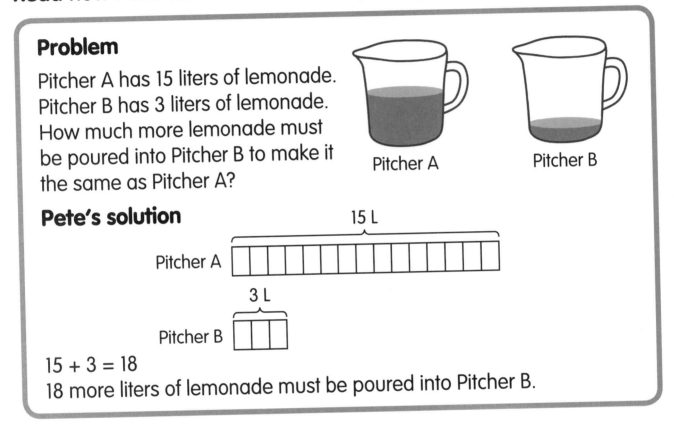

Problem

Pitcher A has 15 liters of lemonade. Pitcher B has 3 liters of lemonade. How much more lemonade must be poured into Pitcher B to make it the same as Pitcher A?

Pitcher A   Pitcher B

Pete's solution

15 L

Pitcher A

3 L

Pitcher B

15 + 3 = 18

18 more liters of lemonade must be poured into Pitcher B.

Is Pete's answer correct?

Why or why not?

If his answer is not correct, then find the correct answer.

Draw a bar model to explain your reasoning.

Put On Your Thinking Cap!

Challenging Practice

Look at the pictures.

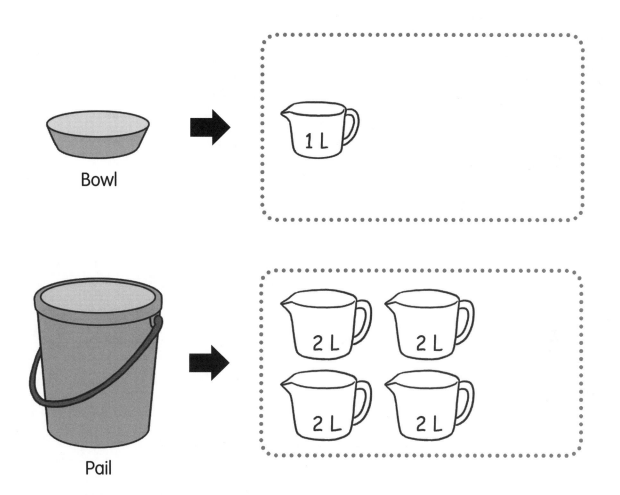

Bowl

1 L

Pail

2 L 2 L
2 L 2 L

a. How many bowls of water does it take to fill each 2-liter pitcher?

_____ bowls

b. How many bowls of water does it take to fill the pail?

_____ bowls

Put On Your Thinking Cap!

Problem Solving

Jasmine is a scientist.
She found a new liquid called Liquid X.
On the first day, she made 2 liters of Liquid X.
On the second day, she made 1 liter more of Liquid X than on the first day.
Every day, she made 1 liter more than the day before.

What was the volume of Liquid X she made on the fifth day?

Try **making a list**.

Chapter Review/Test

Vocabulary

Fill in the blanks with words from the box.

volume	less	liters	more

1. The _____ is the amount of liquid in a container.

2. The volume of a liquid can be measured in _____.

3.

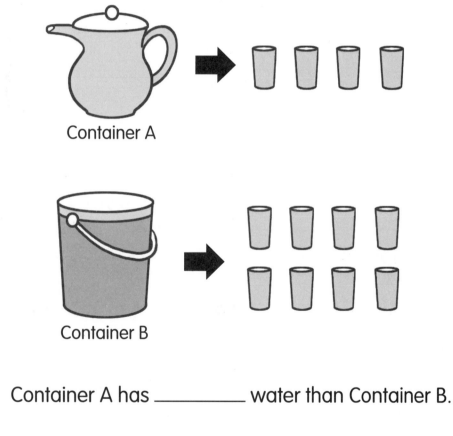

Container A

Container B

a. Container A has _____ water than Container B.

b. Container B has _____ water than Container A.

Concepts and Skills
Fill in the blanks.

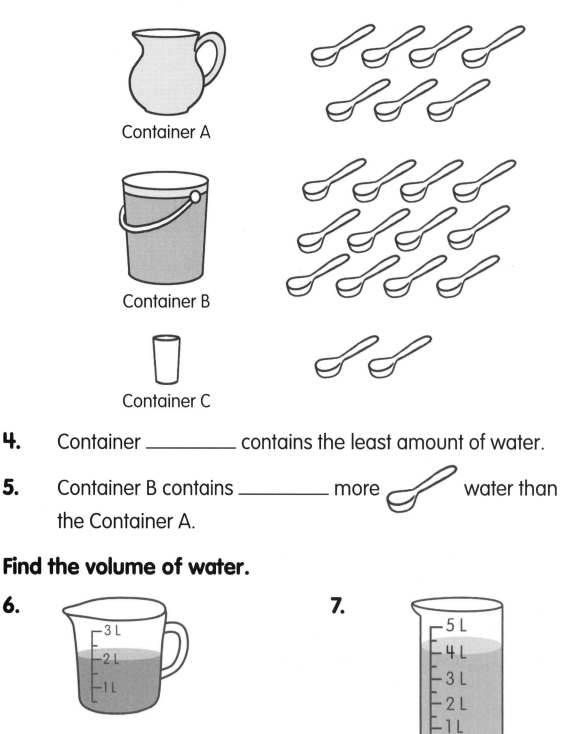

Container A

Container B

Container C

4. Container _____ contains the least amount of water.

5. Container B contains _____ more water than the Container A.

Find the volume of water.

6.

_____ L

7.

_____ L

Name: _____ **Date:** _____

Find the volume of water.

8.

_____ L

9.

_____ L

Problem Solving

Solve.
Use bar models to help you.

10. Mr. Gomez makes 7 liters of apple juice for a party.
He also makes 4 liters of orange juice.
How much juice does he make for the party?

He makes _____ liters of juice for the party.

11. A tank has 13 liters of water.
Lila uses 5 liters of water from the tank.
How much water is left in the tank?

_____ liters of water are left in the tank.

12. 12 liters of water are in a barrel.
Mr. Lopez pours 3 more liters of water into the barrel.
Then he uses 7 liters of water from the barrel to water trees.
How much water is left in the barrel?

_____ liters of water are left in the barrel.

13. A tub can hold 15 liters of water.
2 pails with 6 liters of water in each pail are poured into the tub.
How much more water is needed to fill the tub?

_____ more liters of water are needed to fill the tub.

Cumulative Review
for Chapters 7 to 9

Concepts and Skills

Fill in the blank.

1. Which is longer, 3 meters or 5 meters? _____ m

Measure the pencils.
Then fill in the blanks.

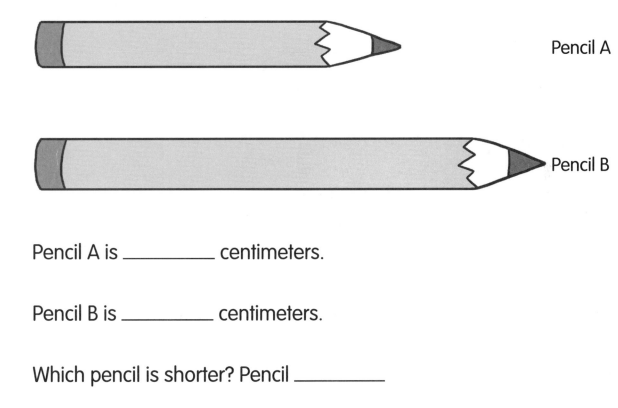

Pencil A

Pencil B

2. Pencil A is _____ centimeters.

3. Pencil B is _____ centimeters.

4. Which pencil is shorter? Pencil _____

5. How much shorter is it? _____ cm

Draw. Then label.

6. Draw a line 7 centimeters long.
Label it Line X.

7. Draw a line 4 centimeters longer than Line X.
Label it Line Y.

Fill in the blanks.

8.

The books have a mass of _____ kilograms.

9.

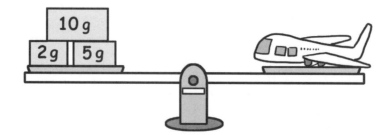

The toy airplane has a mass of _____ grams.

Fill in the blanks.

10. The chicken has a mass of _____ grams.

11. The duck has a mass of _____ grams.

12. Which is lighter? _____

13. How much lighter is it? _____ g

Fill in the blank.

14.

What is the mass of the bag of rice? _____ kg

Look at the pictures.
Then fill in the blank.

15.

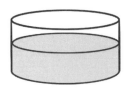

Container A   Container B

Containers A and B are the same size.

Which container has a greater volume of water? Container _____

Fill in the blanks.

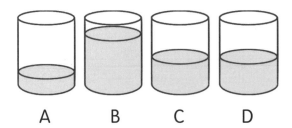

A   B   C   D

Containers A, B, C, and D are the same size.

16. Which container has the most water? Container _____

17. Container _____ contains the same amount as Container _____.

Find the volume of water in each container.

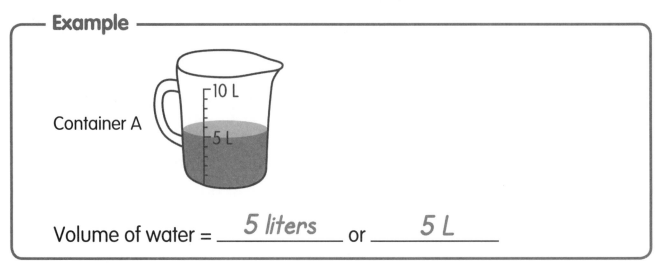

— **Example** —

Container A

┌10 L

┌5 L

Volume of water = ___5 liters___ or ___5 L___

240   Cumulative Review for Chapters 7 to 9

18.

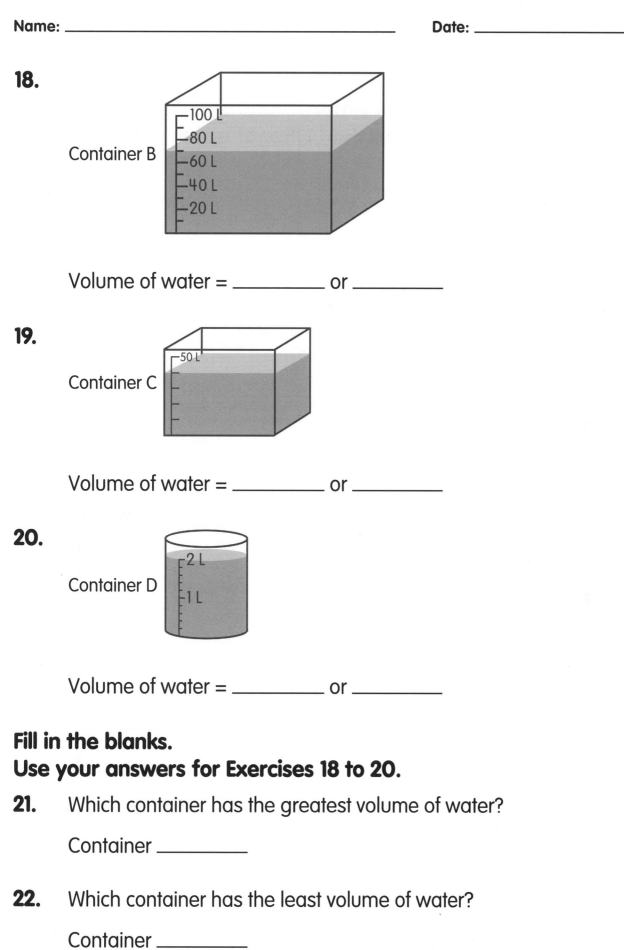

Container B

100 L
80 L
60 L
40 L
20 L

Volume of water = _____ or _____

19.

Container C

50 L

Volume of water = _____ or _____

20.

Container D

2 L
1 L

Volume of water = _____ or _____

Fill in the blanks.
Use your answers for Exercises 18 to 20.

21.   Which container has the greatest volume of water?

Container _____

22.   Which container has the least volume of water?

Container _____

Look at the pictures.
The containers are filled with water.
Which containers contain less than 1 liter of water each?
Circle each answer.

23.

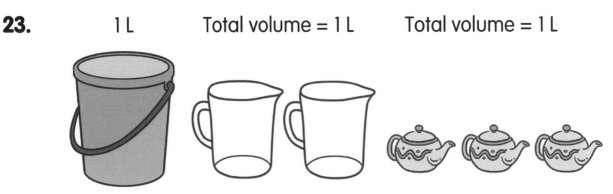

1 L   Total volume = 1 L   Total volume = 1 L

Problem Solving

Solve.
Draw bar models to help you.

24.   Mrs. Kim's empty suitcase has a mass of 5 kilograms.
After she packs some books into the suitcase, her suitcase has
a mass of 21 kilograms.
What is the mass of the books?

The mass of the books is _____ kilograms.

25. Seth has a ball of string.
He uses 35 centimeters of string to decorate his scrapbook.
He uses another 78 centimeters of string to decorate a gift.
  a. How much string does he use in all?
  b. If he had 200 centimeters of string at first, how much string does he have now?

  a. He uses _____ centimeters of string in all.

  b. He has _____ centimeters of string now.

26. Tania's hand puppet has a mass of 440 grams.
It is 120 grams heavier than Hector's hand puppet.
What is the total mass of the two hand puppets?

The total mass of the two hand puppets is _____ grams.

27. A tank contains 65 liters of oil.
Another 15 liters of oil are added.
Later, 40 liters are poured out.
What is the volume of oil in the tank in the end?

The volume of oil in the tank in the end is _____ liters.

28. Sarah sells 27 liters of milk in the morning.
She sells another 8 liters of milk in the afternoon.
Ray sells 48 liters of milk.
   a. Who sells more milk?
   b. How much more?

   a. _____ sells more milk.

   b. _____ sells _____ more liters of milk.

Mid-Year Review

Test Prep

Multiple Choice

Fill in the circle next to the correct answer.

1. Which shows three hundred four?

    Ⓐ 34   Ⓑ 304   Ⓒ 340   Ⓓ 344

2. Which number is shown in the chart?

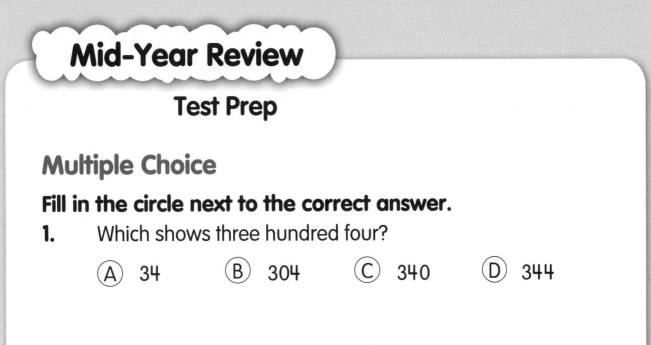

Hundreds	Tens	Ones

    Ⓐ 450   Ⓑ 405   Ⓒ 350   Ⓓ 315

3. Continue the pattern.

    540, 650, 760, 870, _____

    Ⓐ 890   Ⓑ 950   Ⓒ 980   Ⓓ 1,000

4. Add the two numbers shown on the chart.

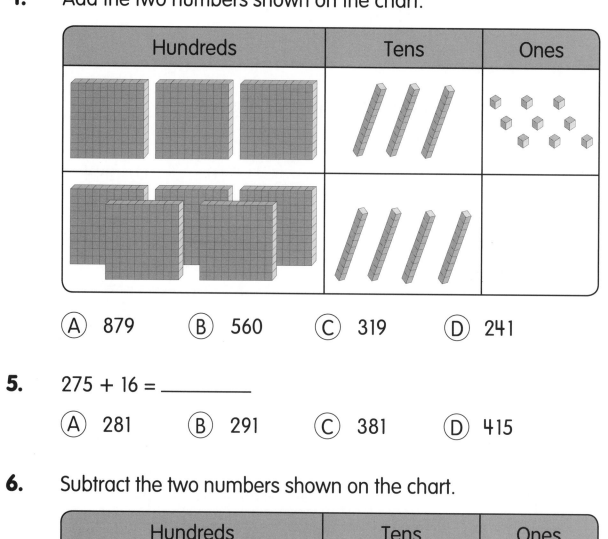

Hundreds	Tens	Ones

A) 879 B) 560 C) 319 D) 241

5. 275 + 16 = _____

A) 281 B) 291 C) 381 D) 415

6. Subtract the two numbers shown on the chart.

Hundreds	Tens	Ones

A) 488 B) 367 C) 246 D) 121

7. Subtract.

$$
\begin{array}{r}
5\ 4\ 7 \\
-\ 2\ 5\ 4 \\
\hline
\end{array}
$$

Ⓐ 801   Ⓑ 393   Ⓒ 313   Ⓓ 293

8. Use these digits.

[2] [7] [5]

Make the greatest 3-digit number.
Then make the least 3-digit number.
Then subtract the two numbers.

Ⓐ 587   Ⓑ 505   Ⓒ 495   Ⓓ 477

9. Darren has 86 marbles.
Max has 74 marbles.
How many marbles do they have in all?

Ⓐ 12   Ⓑ 86   Ⓒ 150   Ⓓ 160

10. Felix has $125.
He uses $70 to buy a pair of shoes.
How much does he have left?

Ⓐ $195   Ⓑ $87   Ⓒ $75   Ⓓ $55

11. Look at the picture.

How many flowers are there?

(A) 7 + 5   (B) 7 × 5   (C) 5 × 2   (D) 5 × 10

12. The length of a placemat is about _____.

(A) 40 cm   (B) 40 m   (C) 1 cm   (D) 1 m

13.

This is the ribbon.

These are the two metersticks, set end-to-end.

What is the length of the ribbon?

(A) 1 cm   (B) 1 m   (C) 2 cm   (D) 2 m

14. Letoya buys 35 books on Monday.
She buys 21 books on Tuesday.
She sells 40 of these books.
How many books does she have left?

(A) 14   (B) 16   (C) 56   (D) 96

15. A carton of milk has a mass of 450 grams.
Two cartons are put into a box with a mass of 37 grams.
What is the total mass of the cartons and the box?

(A) 413 g   (B) 863 g   (C) 937 g   (D) 974 g

Short Answer

Read the questions carefully.
Write your answers in the space provided.

16. Write 386 in words.

_____

17. Write 520 in expanded form.

_____

18. Order the numbers from greatest to least.

⎡609⎤   ⎡712⎤   ⎡699⎤   ⎡543⎤

_____, _____, _____, _____
 greatest   least

19. Add 438 and 156. _____

$$\begin{array}{r} 4\ 3\ 8 \\ +\ 1\ 5\ 6 \\ \hline \end{array}$$

20. Subtract 17 from 831. _____

21.   Subtract 284 from 861.   _____

22.   Fill in the blanks.

$7 \times 2 =$ _____ $2 \times 7 =$ _____

23.   What is the length of Drawing A? _____ cm

_____ Drawing A

24.   What is the mass of the vegetables?

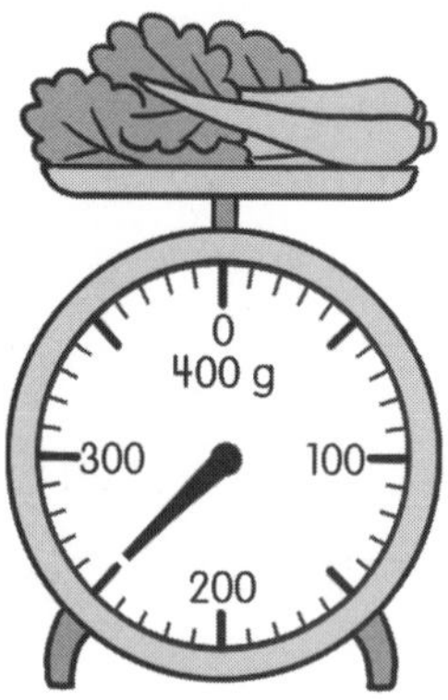

_____ g

25. Fill in the blank with *more than* or *less than*.

The container has _____ 1 liter of water.

26. The Recycling Committee has $746.
They raise $198 more.
How much do they have now?

$ _____

27. In a game, the Green Team scored 270 points.
The Yellow Team scored 363 points.
How many more points did the Yellow Team score
than the Green Team?

_____ points

28. Gina has 200 beads.
94 of the beads are red.
The rest are yellow.
How many yellow beads does Gina have?
Complete the bar model.
Then find the answer.

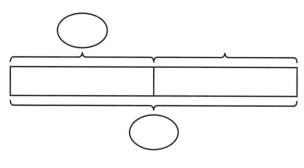

Gina has _____ yellow beads.

29. 138 cars and 27 vans are in a parking lot.
How many vehicles are there in all?
Draw a bar model.
Then find the answer.

There are _____ vehicles in all.

30. The mass of a bottle of hot sauce is 2 kilograms.

2 kg   2 kg   2 kg   2 kg   2 kg   2 kg   2 kg   2 kg   2 kg

What is the mass of 9 bottles?

The mass is _____ kilograms.

31. Eva has 40 crayons.
She gives them to her friends to be shared equally.
Each friend receives 5 crayons.
How many friends are there?

There are _____ friends.

Extended Response

Solve.

Show your work.

32. The Finch family has 352 books.

The Perez family has 168 more books than the Finch family.

    a.   How many books does the Perez family have?

    b.   How many books do the families have in all?

    a.   The Perez family has _____ books.

    b.   The families have _____ books in all.

33. Tasha has 249 cards.

Tim has 53 fewer cards than Tasha.

Lee has 79 more cards than Tim.

How many cards does Lee have?

Lee has _____ cards.

34. Mikayla has 5 strings of beads.
Each string has 4 beads on it.
Mikayla divides her beads into 2 strings of beads.
  a. How many beads does Mikayla have in all?
  b. How many beads are there on each string in the end?

  a. Mikayla has _____ beads in all.

  b. There are _____ beads on each string in the end.

35. Kory has 58 marbles.
Dan has 239 marbles.
  a. How many marbles do they have in all?
  b. What is the difference in the number of marbles between
     Kory and Dan?

  a. They have _____ marbles in all.

  b. The difference in the number of marbles between Kory

     and Dan is _____ centimeters.

36. Mrs. Baibera made 60 cookies.
She gave 14 cookies to Mr. Patterson.
She gave another 13 cookies to her son.
How many cookies are left?

$$
\begin{array}{r}
\overset{5}{\cancel{6}}\overset{10}{\cancel{0}} \\
-\ 1\ 4 \\
\hline
4\ 6
\end{array}
$$

_46_ cookies are left.

37. Ling mixes 120 cups of lemonade in the morning.
She mixes 93 cups of lemonade in the afternoon.

  a. How many cups of lemonade does she mix in all?
  b. She sells 207 cups of lemonade.
  How many cups of lemonade does she have left?

$$
\begin{array}{r}
120 \\
93 \\
+\quad\ \ \\
\hline
213
\end{array}
$$

  a. She mixes _213_ cups of lemonade in all.

  b. She has _6_ cups of lemonade left.